making it
big

the diary of a broadway musical

barbara isenberg

limelight editions
new york

FARCA

First Limelight Edition November 1996

Manufactured in the United States of America

Library of Congress Cataloging-in-Publication Data

Isenberg, Barbara.
    Making It Big : the diary of a Broadway musical /
    by Barbara Isenberg.

    ISBN 0-87910-088-5
    1. Shire, David. Big. I. Title.
    ML410.S52556I84 1996
    782.1'4—dc20   96-43721
                                          CIP
                                          MN

To the memory of my parents, Florence and Harry
Isenberg, who first took me to the theater.

CONTENTS

PROLOGUE

Attempting a new Broadway musical is like trying to house-break a dinosaur, says playwright Larry Gelbart. The effort is enormous, especially if weighed against the odds of success.

If the odds were poor when Gelbart's *City of Angels* opened on Broadway in 1989, they looked even worse in 1995 when I began this book. Although audiences still adored large-scale musicals, whether on Broadway or recycled for hometown consumption, fewer and fewer new domestic ventures have been successful. As the once-great American art form was further colonized by Andrew Lloyd Webber, the natives responded by reviving past glories.

After nearly 20 years of covering musical theater for the *Los Angeles Times*, I questioned just what made the traditional American musical so cumbersome and its fate so imperiled. Is there something wrong with the form itself? And who are the people who refuse to abandon the legacy of *Oklahoma!, Guys and Dolls* and *Cabaret?*

Upon learning that the hit film *Big* was headed for Broadway and realizing that I'd often interviewed many of the key players, I saw the chance to watch firsthand as an ambitious,

high-profile new musical took shape through auditions, readings, production meetings, budget sessions and out-of-town tryouts. I wrote to the musical's director, Mike Ockrent—someone I'd written about when he directed *Me and My Girl*—and with his cooperation then met with other members of the creative and production teams. While they would have no control over the final telling of their story, all agreed to give me full cooperation and access.

Big's odyssey to Broadway has been both arduous and costly—at $10.3 million, it is among the most expensive musicals in Broadway history. Since 1989, when the show's collaborators first thought about adapting *Big* as a musical, composer David Shire and lyricist Richard Maltby, Jr., have written 58 songs. Book writer John Weidman has turned out enough script pages to make a stack of papers half as tall as he is. The show's leading lady, Crista Moore, had to learn five different opening ballads, sometimes overnight, and the leading man, Daniel Jenkins, had major knee surgery just weeks before opening night.

Postponed from fall, 1995, to spring, 1996, the musical plowed around, over and through obstacles at nearly every turn. Its out of town tryout was moved from Boston in summer to Detroit in winter. Plagued by set problems, unappreciated by local critics, *Big* found in the Midwest a harrowing preview of future struggles on Broadway for good notices, audiences and Tony awards.

Ockrent and company demonstrate that with musicals, as with dinosaurs, you must appreciate their scale, do your best to tame them, then get out of the way.

Hard work and vaulting dreams are not always rewarded.

PART ONE:
BEGINNINGS

"There is this big mass audience out there that doesn't go to theater.... Beauty and the Beast was the first show many of them went to, and Big could be the second."

— James B. Freydberg, producer,
April 6, 1995

BEGINNINGS

1989

Aᴄᴛʀᴇss Didi Conn has a few hours to kill in a suburban California hotel room. Her husband, composer David Shire, is away on business, and she decides to watch a pay-per-view television showing of *Big*, a film she remembers fondly.

She's charmed again by Tom Hanks as a 12-year-old trapped in a grown man's body, awkwardly romancing Elizabeth Perkins and exuberantly dancing with Robert Loggia on a giant piano keyboard at F.A.O. Schwarz. She registers anew the fantasy, the humor, the tenderness. Then she registers its potential: *Big* could well become the hit Broadway musical that Shire and his long-time writing partner, lyricist Richard Maltby, Jr., have been searching for. The minute Shire gets back to the room, she starts teasing him: does he want a really "Big" idea for Broadway, a really "Big" show?

Of course he does. Since meeting at Yale their first year of college, Maltby and Shire have yearned to follow in the tradition of Rodgers and Hammerstein, Lerner and Loewe. They wrote two musicals—*Cyrano* and *Grand Tour*—even before they graduated in 1959. Their actors included such classmates as Dick Cavett, Austin Pendleton, Gretchen Cryer and A. Bartlett Giamatti, a future Yale president. John Badham, who would later direct such films as *Saturday Night Fever*, was their stage manager, and Christopher Porterfield, today assistant managing editor of *Time* Magazine, did orchestrations and played clarinet in their band.

Theirs was the dream of an entire theatrical generation and one they have pursued over time with some success. Their 1977 Off Broadway revue, *Starting Here, Starting Now*, and 1983 musical *Baby*, which ran eight months on Broadway, have had hundreds of productions worldwide and are still playing in one city or another.

Each has also done well individually. Maltby, who won a Tony for directing *Ain't Misbehavin'*, also directed Broadway productions of not just *Baby* but also Andrew Lloyd Webber's *Song and Dance.* Shire won an Oscar for the song, "It Goes

7

Like It Goes," for the 1979 film, *Norma Rae*, and has written dozens of television and film scores over the years.

But writing film scores is writing background music, Conn says. Her husband should be writing foreground.

She doesn't let up. "It was hard for David to admit he wanted a big hit. Maybe it's hard for everybody. People are afraid of something that could be too commercial. You want to win the World Series and the Academy Award. You want to be Michael Jordan. Should that be something to be ashamed of?"

Shire takes the idea to Maltby and to James Freydberg, the man who produced *Baby*. Freydberg has been a gambler of sorts since he was 21; his father handed him $1,000 to build a future, and he bet $800 of it—successfully—on a horse race. Both Maltby and Freydberg are skeptical but not uninterested.

Conn meanwhile approaches film producer Laurence Mark, whom she's known since the late '70s, when she was playing Frenchy in *Grease* and he was running publicity at Paramount. Aware that he keeps an apartment in New York, she has a hunch he might like to produce plays there. And, she recalls, "Larry got really excited. It wasn't too hard to fan his flame."

Shire and Mark meet for lunch. Mark, who was a senior production executive on the film, is not just interested but willing to call the film's producer James Brooks, a friend and colleague. Brooks is receptive, and Mark initiates discussions with Twentieth Century Fox about obtaining rights to the property.

While Freydberg's skepticism eases somewhat once rights look possible, Maltby is not yet convinced that *Big* will work as a musical. "A kid makes an absolutely casual wish and once he gets to be big, all he wants to do is get to be small again," says Maltby. "He meets a girl and they have a little bit of a something or other, but then he goes home.

"The movie didn't have a real plot. It was held together by the charm of a performance that really reads onscreen, and its best moments didn't seem translatable to the stage. The biggest moment, the one that makes you think, 'Oh, I want to

make it a musical,' is the keyboard moment, and it's already been done. You can't just trot it out on the stage and have everybody say how wonderful it is."

As the year winds down, Maltby is busy launching *Miss Saigon*, on which he is co-lyricist. Shire is enmeshed in his television and film scores. Their new revue, *Closer than Ever*, opens in November Off Broadway at the Cherry Lane Theatre, and *Big* essentially languishes.

1990

Shire mentions *Big* to book writer John Weidman, collaborator with Stephen Sondheim on *Pacific Overtures* and *Assassins*. They had talked earlier about working together one day, but the timing is wrong now. Weidman is otherwise engaged.

1991

Maltby is more open to the idea of *Big*, and the songwriters review a "wish list" of book writers, people they'd always wanted to write musicals with—among them Wendy Wasserstein, John Patrick Shanley, and Donald Margulies.

"The book writer is the heart and soul of a musical," says Maltby. "Things have to deliver at certain moments, and there isn't time for evocative dialogue. You often have two or three sentences, and they have to make the plot turn and be funny and subtle and witty and dramatic. But the book writer gets very, very little attention [unless] the show's terrible. If it's wonderful, it's because of those great songs. Ah, and there's some interesting little dialogue."

Maltby and Shire talk with both playwrights and television writers. One potential bookwriting team keeps them dangling so long that Weidman becomes available again. He and Shire discuss *Big*, although Weidman is initially ambivalent. "It's awkward to move from a film to the stage anyway," the playwright says. "Why do again something that was done so well the first time?"

Everyone Shire talks to seems to love the idea, Weidman says, but "everyone I talk to says it's a shitty idea."

What finally snares Weidman is the same thing that eventually snares Maltby: both men see a larger tale to tell. Weidman watches the film again with his wife, Lila Coleburn, a psychologist, and finds in it "one of the nine elemental human stories" of how we grow up wanting to skip the hard parts in life but knowing we shouldn't. Turning that story into musical theater, he says, seemed both possible and worthwhile.

"All kids want to grow up," says Maltby. "They hate being what they are and want to be grownups when they can do all the other things. There's some central mythology in this story that isn't described by the script but is evoked by the whole. John defined that and set us on our course. With that in hand, we could begin to define a stage version. And every time we went astray, we would always come back to it."

1992

The three men take a long weekend in Connecticut. They bring with them not just the final film script (which won Oscar nominations for screenwriting partners Gary Ross and Anne Spielberg) but also several earlier versions to see what was cut. They decide they can still walk away from the project at any time, but the only way they'll find out if *Big* can be a musical is to try to write *Big: The Musical*.

Here and elsewhere, they outline their show, scene by scene, trying to figure out who their characters are, what they should sing and when they should sing it. Musicals are keenly dependent upon structure. "Yes, you've got to have great songs and well-written scenes," explains Shire, "but it is amazing how many great songs don't work if they are not set up right or if they are not the song that the audience wants to hear at that point. The scene or song can fail because information wasn't set up three scenes before."

Maltby, meanwhile, is obsessed with all those memorable close-ups of Tom Hanks; the ingratiating actor makes faces, smiles winningly, eats baby corn as if it were corn on the cob.

10

The film has no action-slowing dialogue about Josh's inner anguish.

"The movie doesn't have a single introspective sentence in it," says Maltby, "and lyrics are introspective moments. John can write scintillating dialogue and move the action along. David can write music which is evocative and does whatever music can do. But someone has to dig into a child's brain and give all that stuff words."

Maltby wants to be that someone, the one who expresses the emotions that aren't usually articulated. "It's the moment when a girl you have seen a hundred times passes in front of you, and suddenly you're tongue-tied. You're not quite sure what the feelings are and where they're going to lead. That's the primal age, the end of childhood and the beginning of adulthood."

So emerges "I Want to Know." It is the song that will lead into the show's key romantic interlude, and one which Maltby feels captures both the innocence and hushed expectancy of a boy confronting sex for the first time.

"All shows fall apart in the creative process at one point or another," Maltby says. "You lose sight of what you're doing, and you don't know whether it's worth going forward or not. Then something holds you to it. When Lerner and Loewe were writing *My Fair Lady*, and got the idea for 'The Rain In Spain,' they knew it could work on the stage. As soon as 'I Want to Know' happened, I knew that we could write something for a 13-year-old that was worth singing about."

Their show has found its anchor.

1993

Work continues. "More than anything else, we found ourselves doing it," says Weidman. "I don't know if there even was actually a moment where we decided to do it. It just was happening."

In November, Maltby and Shire perform chunks of the score for potential *Big* producer Kenneth Feld one day, for potential producer Kenneth Greenblatt the next. Both are interested.

Feld, based in Vienna, Virginia, runs Irvin Feld & Kenneth Feld Productions, Inc., producer of Ringling Bros. and Barnum & Bailey circus, Disney ice shows, Siegfried & Roy and other live entertainment around the world. Feld likes both the property and its marketing potential: based on a film that grossed $120 million in the U.S. and $44 million abroad, the musical is family-oriented and could have wide international appeal. He also has a solid working relationship with Freydberg, with whom he'd earlier co-produced *Fool Moon*.

Feld calls it a business decision, but it is much more than that for Greenblatt, a printed fabrics manufacturer who has invested in 11 Broadway shows and who will eventually bring in $5 million of his own and others' money. A state wrestling champion when he was in college, and a man given to such phrases as "This is easy, textiles is hard," Greenblatt will become the show's most ardent cheerleader.

1994

Sunday, January 16, 1994

Choreographer Susan Stroman and director Mike Ockrent hear the score for the first time at Shire's Greenwich Village apartment.

The energetic English director and kinetic blonde choreographer have had great success with *Crazy for You* and are just back from launching a Toronto production of the Gershwin musical. Before *Crazy for You*, Ockrent directed *Me and My Girl*, which played more than three years on Broadway and will run eight years in London's West End. Stroman, in turn, recently choreographed Harold Prince's revival of *Show Boat* in Toronto, an achievement which will win her another Tony award when the show moves on to New York.

Stroman and Ockrent, who live together (and will marry during the course of the show's odyssey), are carrying music and scripts for *A Christmas Carol*, a new musical based on the Dickens classic, which is set for the 5,600-seat Paramount Theatre at Madison Square Garden later this year. But like everyone else in this business, they are looking for their next

project before completing the current one.

Both have some reservations about *Big*. Stroman, for instance, has high expectations since she is a major fan of Maltby and Shire's music, but while she's climbing all the steps up to Shire's rooftop study, she's worrying about how much dance they envision for the show. Are they seeing it with a lot of movement?

"I react to music visually," Stroman says, "and a lot of people who write music do not. I didn't know their process or anything about them. I didn't know how to react. I told them how great the songs sounded and they did. But I knew the story and didn't know quite how I'd fit in. If they just needed someone to move actors from one ballad to another, they didn't need me."

Ockrent, who hasn't yet seen the film *Big*, has long wanted to direct a musical set in his own time. But he, too, is skeptical. "When you take a well-known contemporary movie, one that is much-loved, you are courting disaster from the beginning," he says. "People come in with so many preconceptions about it. It feels like a cheaper idea, whereas when you take an obscure movie, that has a better feel."

The director had spent three years writing a novel, *Running Down Broadway*, about people who do what he does. His fictional director says such things as, "Working on a musical is like swimming through shark-infested waters with a bleeding toe." His fictional producer figures, "People go to musicals to hear music and cry. For philosophy, they go to college."

At the end of the meeting, both Stoman and Ockrent are intrigued, although not willing to commit themselves. Stroman is initially charmed more by the authors than by their proposal, she admits, "but it was also clear they wanted to make it a theater piece and not just a screenplay that someone shoved music into."

Shire is disappointed but understands their reaction. "You always hope when you play something for somebody they are going to jump up and down like in the movies and go, 'Oh God, that's it, let's get that show on as fast as possible,'" says the composer. "Seasoned theater professionals don't do that;

we know how hard it is to come up with anything that works. But they liked us and they liked the basic material."

Friday, February 11, 1994

Ockrent has now seen the film and feels the musical is too similar; they must move away from it and create a separate theater piece. The first act is 85 pages long, more than 50 scenes and nearly every beat of the film. "You have to put it in definable scenes," he tells the writers. "This isn't a huge epic adventure like *Les Misérables*."

Arguing that the plot doesn't really begin until Josh Baskin meets Susan Lawrence, Ockrent compresses early scenes and songs. He scraps 25 pages, speeding up the time it takes to set up the story, establish Josh as a likeable kid and get him to his wish.

The director also postpones the seduction scene. Maltby, Shire and Weidman choose to end the first act with Josh singing "I Want to Know" and being led by Susan into the bedroom. Ockrent disagrees: the seduction scene has to wait until the second act.

There are two basic romantic themes, Ockrent says. Boy has girl, boy loses girl, boy finds girl again—the plot of *Me and My Girl* and *Crazy for You*. The second is the delayed sex plot of *Big*. "They have to wait and sleep together as far into the second act as possible," explains the director, "so there is still some sort of dramatic tension."

Monday, May 2, 1994

Maltby and Shire go to the Shubert Theatre to see *Crazy for You* again now that they're informally working with Stroman and Ockrent. The composer and lyricist discover they are both thinking how wonderful it would be if they could do *Big* there. "It's not the most perfect theater," says Maltby, "but it's the one that once in life, you'd want to have a show playing in."

Wednesday, June 1, 1994

Big's first invited reading is planned for June 19. Ockrent

likes to have professional actors read and sing through a script so the authors can see how a show looks on its feet. The writing team likes readings because they create needed deadlines.

As so often happens in theater, Ockrent has given considerable time to the project but is not yet committed. "It is amazing how so many things go on in the theater collaboratively without contracts," Shire says. "People just try everybody out and see what the fit is. Then when it happens officially, it all seems to happen at once."

Sunday, June 19, 1994

A dozen actors perform the show's first reading for maybe two dozen family members, friends and potential producers at a midtown rehearsal studio.

Rewrites will follow the reading. So will more rewrites. Maltby compares all the polishing to what happens when you change a tire. You tighten one bolt, then another, then have to keep going round and round the wheel. You fix one thing and something else has to be fixed.

Among the fixes will be a change in which character sings the key song, "I Want to Know." While the song was written for the adult Josh, Maltby and Ockrent have been talking about a possible duet between the young Josh and adult Josh. Then, at the end of today's reading, Maltby heads over to the boy playing young Josh, "privately, because I was afraid of what I might hear, and I asked him if these were thoughts he might have. He said, 'Oh, definitely, but I would never tell anyone.'"

Convinced now of the power of a duet, Ockrent sets the song up that way through the show's remaining readings. (In time, it will become a solo for young Josh.)

Tuesday, December 6, 1994

A second reading is scheduled for later this month, and the collaborators rework their show for several days at Ockrent and Stroman's London flat. Days are so long they call the place Camp Ockrent.

Talking with Stroman, the writers also come up with the notion of dancing Susan and Josh into bed. Then, working

through their heroine's childhood, they start grilling Stroman about her own teens. When she replies that essentially all she can remember is dancing all the time, something clicks. Or as Shire puts it: "It was worth flying to London just to hear her say that."

Maltby and Shire return to New York and write "Dancing All the Time," the song that will lead first into "I Want to Know," then into the bedroom.

Saturday, December 17, 1994

Second reading. Ockrent now feels ready to involve a design team. He invites his *Crazy for You* collaborators: set designer Robin Wagner, costume designer William Ivey Long, lighting designer Paul Gallo, musical director Paul Gemignani and others.

Stakes are high. Weidman feels this is also their final audition for Ockrent "to see if the work we had all done together made him want to do the show. It was never said explicitly and didn't need to be. And I had absolutely no problem with it."

The gamble pays off. Stroman, Ockrent and the design team sign on. Feld and Greenblatt join producers Freydberg and Mark.

Feld tells Freydberg not to worry now about financing the show. "I said, 'Let's take our time and make sure we can do it right,'" says Feld. "We decided on an $8.5 million budget but put aside $10 million so we had a cushion to create a great marketing campaign. I said I would guarantee it, so the time could be devoted to refining the product, as opposed to everybody scrambling and looking for money."

They pull out their calendars and decide to shoot for an opening in early October, 1995. In mid-October, Stroman and Ockrent have to start rehearsing *A Christmas Carol*. Freydberg has a movie commitment. Weidman has another project with Sondheim.

"We decided, 'Let's go,'" Shire says. "We'll stay up a few nights."

1995

Friday, January 20, 1995

Maltby and Shire narrate and perform a chunk of their show for New York theater owners. They are at Shubert offices in the morning, Nederlander offices in the afternoon.

Thursday, January 26, 1995, Sherman Oaks, California

Maltby and Shire take their act to the West Coast. Friends come by Shire's suburban Los Angeles home this afternoon for a rehearsal of tonight's presentation to Twentieth Century Fox and other movie people; they need to know that the musical won't bring shame upon them and their film. With Shire at the piano (and sometimes singing with Maltby), composer and lyricist perform a 45-minute sampler that sweeps in eight songs plus narration. Shire closes the afternoon event by admitting he is more nervous in front of friends than he expects to be tonight.

Friday, February 10 and Saturday, February 11, 1995, Los Angeles

Auditions at the Coronet Theatre. Maltby, Shire, Ockrent, Stroman, Weidman, conductor Paul Gemignani and casting director Vinnie Liff are in town to see local stage, television and film actors.

The weekend's call is for the five principal adult roles: Josh Baskin, the show's lead, which requires an actor with the appeal of Tom Hanks who won't remind audiences of Hanks; Susan Lawrence, the love interest; George MacMillan, the toy company president, which may be a star cameo; adversary Paul Seymour, which calls for a guy to be mean and unpleasant onstage; and Mrs. Baskin, Josh's mother, a small role that will get smaller later.

Actors enter the auditorium one at a time. They greet the *Big* contingent, walk to the stage, hand music they've selected to an accompanist, then sing. Casting assistants hand them "a side" of a few script pages, which most have already seen and prepared, and perform it with them.

One scene involves a fight between Josh and Paul, and the casting assistant takes a real battering from actors demonstrating their ability to emote anger. Josh has to confess to Susan in one scene that he is only 13, then in another scene, throw up caviar. Susan, in turn, has to listen to his confession and side-step the caviar.

Jon Cypher, who played the Police Chief in *Hill Street Blues* and the eccentric General in *Major Dad*, reads and sings so well that Stroman rushes up to have him try a dance number. He can't. Hurt his knee 2½ years ago. (*Big* delays long enough for Cypher to have knee surgery, try out again and get the role. More on that later.)

At the end of each day, the decision-makers huddle in two rows of the otherwise empty theater. They review 8x10 glossies and resumes, talking about each actor with the caution of used-car buyers.

They review their notes, their options. Who should they ask to New York for a "callback" or second look? Does an actor sing as well as he acts? Will a particular actress be willing to play the chorus for a chance to stand by for the lead? And can they ask her in such a way that it's an inquiry, not an offer?

Friday, March 3, 1995

First look at the set. The creative team gathers in designer Robin Wagner's studio at 890 Broadway, a theater-oriented building in the Flatiron district where many musicals have auditioned, rehearsed or otherwise taken shape. *Victor/Victoria* and *Big* will both rehearse here this year.

Wagner's place is open and spacious, a sprawling amalgam of design tables, sofas, desks and ficus trees. As the show evolves, his studio will often serve as meeting place for costume, lighting and other design departments.

Today, a scale model of the stage rests in a box about the size of a large television set. Wagner is at the side, moving tiny cardboard people and props on and offstage, and his assistant stands on a ladder moving backdrops and "hangers," hanging pieces, from above. Scene after scene rolls by—a neighborhood, carnival, bus station, Josh's loft, a yuppie apart-

ment. Each scene uses something from the scene before it, creating a series of transformations.

Weidman's questions readily identify him as a worrier, and Ockrent's answers similarly identify him as someone who has dealt with a lot of worriers. Maltby is characteristically enthusiastic, jumping up to shake Wagner's hand and say the set is "everything I imagined or expected, and way beyond anything I imagined or expected."

Yet also clear, even at this point, are author anxieties about surrounding their small tale with such a large frame. Shire frets that the roller coaster seems excessive for a temporary carnival. The director defends the roller coaster, saying that at the opening of the show, they need a strong visual effect. Weidman says they may be overthinking it; how many people will actually wonder if it's too big for a temporary carnival? It stays.

Weidman wants seats in the bus station "to distinguish it from, say, Lebanon," but other concerns seem more serious. The toy lunar module in the loft scene looks as if it came from N.A.S.A., the authors say, and the mini-automobile seems excessive. (Both are later scrapped.) "Will the set dwarf this intimate story?" asks Shire. "Will the story get lost?"

Saturday, March 4, 1995

Rehearsal for the show's third reading. Ockrent reminds the actor playing Josh that Josh may look like an adult, talk like an adult and even act like an adult, but he is a kid. And the actor playing him—whether at this reading, or later, in the actual show—has to remember that.

When Josh learns that girls stuff their training bras with Kleenex, explains Ockrent, "It's something he can't wait to share with the other kids." And once he's sexually experienced, he goes off to meet Susan's friends both over-confident and full of himself. Ockrent turns to the actor playing one of the friends, "And *you* immediately detect an idiot walking through the front door."

Ockrent, who frequently refers to his own 13-year-old son, Ben, has no trouble at all thinking like a kid. He may have directed Strindberg and Sondheim, but physical comedy is

rarely too broad for him. The actor playing Josh pretends to throw up after tasting caviar for the first time, and Ockrent laughs out loud. "When in doubt," he jokes, "put in a vomit scene."

Sunday, March 5, 1995

Third reading. Audience response is less enthusiastic than last December, worrying the authors.

Josh is too passive. "On most musicals, you have a character who in the first five minutes says, 'I want something,' and for the whole evening is trying to get that something," says Shire. "In this musical, a character says right off the bat that he wants to be big, gets his wish immediately and then wants to undo it. After that, he becomes a relatively reactive character, which can be deadly for a musical."

One result is that Susan's interest in Josh seems largely unmotivated. She has to arrive at his apartment, then find it and him magical. Worries Weidman: "All of that was wonderful in the film."

Much of the film's plot and many of its lines have been retained onstage. In both, 12-year-old Josh Baskin is rejected as too small for a carnival ride, a humiliation thrust upon him in front of both his best friend Billy and the lustrous 13-year-old Cynthia Benson. Fleeing, he discovers a Zoltar wish-granting arcade machine and wishes to be big. The next morning he's indeed big, a kid in a grown-up body who scares his mom and has to run away from his sweet New Jersey neighborhood.

Aided by street-wise Billy, Josh lands in New York and F.A.O. Schwarz, where he and toy company owner MacMillan bond while dancing together on a giant-size piano keyboard. Josh's fortunes multiply: he becomes a hot-shot toy executive, acquires a fabulous apartment, charms female colleague Susan Lawrence, has his first sexual experience. But he knows he's still a kid, wants to go home and, after he finds another Zoltar machine, does exactly that.

Same basic plot, onstage and onscreen. But Weidman's script has to accommodate songs, and even Wagner, the man

who designed *Dreamgirls, A Chorus Line* and *City of Angels*, has to draw the line somewhere on locations. Gone are the film's limousine ride, Times Square hotel and other settings. A gym-size trampoline, the device at Josh's apartment that onscreen helps soften Susan, has been replaced by a Magic Castle—a large, castle-shaped inflatable toy that already seems dicey (and will plague them through Detroit).

Stuff just isn't working, and the end of the first act has already emerged as the show's Achilles' heel. "It's the problem of having two acts," says Shire. "You didn't have it with the screenplay."

Monday, March 6, 1995

Press release announces that *Big* will arrive on Broadway next fall after an engagement at the Shubert Theatre in Boston from July 27 through Sept. 2. Official New York opening: October 12 "at a theater to be announced."

Tuesday, March 7, 1995

Weidman is in his office at *Sesame Street*, for which his writing has already won him seven Emmy Awards. The television writing followed several years of writing screenplays that weren't produced, musicals that were, and a college career training to become a lawyer.

Even before he received his degree from Yale Law School, he slid into his father Jerome Weidman's profession by writing the book for *Pacific Overtures*. When Weidman's father was working on the Pulitzer Prize-winning *Fiorello!* in 1959, his 13-year-old son saw it in New Haven, Philadelphia and then New York. "I got to go backstage," Weidman says, "and watching him do what he did was a very heady experience. Probably he lured me into this whether he wanted to or not."

Weidman is still depressed by Sunday's reading. "We had this very positive experience in December," he says. "It was a good day at the theater, as good in its way as Sunday was not. Four minutes into this theatrical event, we were just dead.

"It's not as if, 'Oh, my God, the wheels fell off and we'll never get them back on.' It's like maybe they're the wrong

wheels and maybe we need to change them a little bit. The consensus that what happened Sunday didn't add up to much is easy. What to do about it isn't."

Wednesday, March 8, 1995

Creative team meets at Maltby's office on Upper East Side.

They're analyzing the seduction scene. What exactly would a kid do in this situation? A 30-year-old woman? Should either of them undress onstage? And if someone does go into the bathroom to disrobe, how will the audience hear the conversation? To illustrate his point, Ockrent gets up, leaves the room, closes the door and starts to talk. You can't understand a word he's saying.

Maltby's file drawers are crammed with discarded songs and scripts. Among the detritus: an early script that opened with weird puberty rites featuring Bar Mitzvah boys and African spear-throwers.

When scenes go, so do the songs within them, but Maltby seems philosophical about it. "Mostly songs go away not because they're intrinsically bad, but because the dramatic impulse that supports the song goes away. You could have a song that you just absolutely love, which when it becomes dramatically unnecessary becomes suddenly loathsome. You can't wait until you get it out of the way so the story can go back to being what it now wants to be.

"We are the creators of this show and in charge of where it goes. But we are also servants of the show and we watch it going where it has to go. That's the magic."

Thursday, March 9, 1995

Auditions at John Houseman Theatre on 42nd St. They now have their leading man—Daniel Jenkins—and are looking for their leading lady.

Jenkins was a favorite for Josh early on, and, although he was first suggested by Shire, Liff says, "Dan was so wonderful, we all wished we could take credit for coming up with the idea." The actor, who was nominated for a Tony when he played Huck Finn in *Big River* in 1985, was most

recently on Broadway as Prior Walter, replacing Stephen Spinella in the lead of *Angels in America*. He did well at the readings, and although they kept auditioning better-known actors, says Shire, "We were determined not to cast anyone who wasn't as good as Dan."

Jenkins, 32, is on hand to read with some of the actresses who have been called back today for a second look. He seems very boyish in his khakis, orangish T-shirt, and tennis shoes and readily admits the role "fits like a glove. I don't have to tear my hair out to get into this guy's skin because I feel like his spirit is so close to my spirit."

Sometimes Jenkins sits out in the auditorium with the creative team, but rarely for long; more often, he's leaping onstage to read lines with one of the actresses. Nearly all the women who audition today have played leads in musicals, many on Broadway. The prime contenders for Susan are Crista Moore, who received a Tony nomination in the title role of *Gypsy* a few years ago, and Karen Ziemba, who plays the lead in *Crazy for You* on Broadway—a role Moore played on tour—and who, Maltby says, performed the part of Susan "wonderfully" in the show's first two readings.

Weidman feels that dark-haired, big-eyed Moore "just jumped off the page." The actress also has the vulnerability of her film counterpart Elizabeth Perkins. She is dressed all in black—blazer, fancy shirt, short skirt. She wore the same clothes to her first audition for the part; she thinks the short skirt makes her look sexy and the long blazer sophisticated. She seems very nervous.

Callbacks are tough, Jenkins says later. "Usually in an audition you psyche yourself up for two to five minutes of output. There's enough gas in the tank for that. You're always worse in the callback; the monkey's on your back. You have to be as good as you were last time, which is just about impossible, and you feel like old news already. They've seen all your tricks. Spontaneity is your friend in the first one."

Moore, who had pushed for an audition when her agent felt she wasn't right for the part, says, "I read a lot of scripts and I loved the material." She'd spent considerable time learn-

ing Susan's songs—onstage now, she jokes that it's been "like a marathon"—and it shows. When she sings "Dancing All the Time," it is difficult to imagine anyone else in the role.

Moore and Jenkins also seem believable as a couple. "Something either happens or doesn't happen with someone on a reading, and it definitely happened with her," Jenkins says. "It's called chemistry. Take one man, mix with woman. Add script, shake well, pour on stage. Sit back and judge."

The creative team deliberates, opinions are divided, and they put off a decision. But by the end of the month, they choose Moore.

6:00 pm

Freydberg and Ockrent head down the street to the corner coffee shop. Freydberg is agitated, and he wants to talk to Ockrent alone. It has to do with money, the director knows, and he also knows that money is not the best thing to talk about with your producer.

Freydberg hands Ockrent a big gray envelope. Ockrent opens it and quickly scans page after page of budget breakdown. As Ockrent reads, Freydberg goes on about how expensive everything is. He is showing the budget details to Ockrent, Freydberg explains, because the man who shepherded *Crazy for You* through three years on Broadway and productions in several countries is a director who understands numbers.

They're short on time to get everything done, he tells Ockrent. That's why he's sitting there in a place that sells wine at $2.50 a glass, consuming awful navy bean soup and feeling trapped between a creative team gearing toward a pre-Broadway tryout that summer and a financial team questioning that schedule's fiscal wisdom.

Ockrent looks up from the numbers. "Are you telling me you want to postpone this?"

By way of answer, the producer reaches into his pocket to pull out a piece of yellow lined paper folded to the size of a cigarette pack. Unfolding it slowly, he says, "Here are some reasons why we might."

Freydberg reads through his list. Negotiations aren't done

yet on the set, which will be expensive to build and run. There are script and score problems. He is also concerned that *Crazy for You*, which currently occupies the Shubert Theatre, is still doing well.

"I'm not saying we should postpone," says the producer. "I'm saying I'm a little bit frightened about where we are. I'm under a lot of pressure to have this make sense."

Ockrent can't believe what he's hearing. He, Stroman and several members of *Big*'s technical team have been restructuring their work schedules on *A Christmas Carol* to accommodate *Big*'s Broadway premiere in October. He and Stroman plan to be married on New Year's Eve after both shows open. Originally he had even argued for postponement himself, only to be talked out of it.

The director knows that an October, 1995, opening would become an April, 1996, opening. Other members of the creative team had turned down work based on the earlier schedule. Jenkins let television pilot season lapse, and he has a new baby at home.

The producer, in turn, knows that opening in the fall would make them less dependent on Tony wins. But if they wait, they would at least avoid opening at the same time as Julie Andrews in *Victor/Victoria* and Tommy Tune in *Busker Alley*. "You wouldn't be going head to head against two big star packages," says Freydberg.

It is almost as if Ockrent can see the future. "You don't know what will be there next spring," Ockrent replies. "It's in the laps of the gods, anyway."

Wednesday, March 15, 1995, Hollywood

Freydberg is settling into a new house here in the hills where he can flee New York. Escape the stress. Regroup.

"I'm out here to get away from the pressure," Freydberg admits. "I have three other partners, but in reality, the day-to-day responsibility is falling on my shoulders. From time to time I switch that responsibility to one of my other partners in some way, but I'm the person who does this for a living."

Freydberg, who looks a little like the actor Michael Douglas, is not really happy with any of his alternatives

now. He can push a New York opening this fall without an out-of-town tryout, something that would save about $1.5 million, and *Big* could come in as an $8.5 million show. But nobody else seems to want that, and he could lose Ockrent.

But delaying to accommodate Ockrent's schedule on *A Christmas Carol*—which is what will indeed happen—doesn't look so good either. "When you come in late in the season, and don't win a Tony, you're a loser," Freydberg says. "Only one show can win, and if you're not that winner, you won't even have time to build an audience. If you come in early and don't even get nominated, you're still a winner because you ran the whole season and built an audience."

Freydberg, 55, once senior vice-president for institutional trading at Drexel, has been a theater producer for 24 years. He's never produced anything on this scale before—few people have—but he already knows that being the point man can be hazardous to your health. Midwife to the dreams of others, he has to be there if they need him but also stay out of their way.

"The producer has to be able to wear a lot of different hats and be able to listen," says Freydberg, answering one more New York call on his cellular phone. "To the emotional anxieties of the other producers. To the director's demands. The writer's demands. The costume designer.

"Everybody has those moments when they get scared, and one of the things a producer has to do is to be strong through that period and not fall into despair himself. But sometimes you do: Are we going to get all the money? Is this really a budget that's going to work out? Am I being supportive in a way that's constructive? The pressure and the strain of doing this is enormous."

Tuesday, April 4, 1995
10:15 am

Wagner's studio. He is meeting with special effects designer Gregory Meeh. Among topics under discussion: A spark-gen-

26

erating skateboard. Wild Thunder roller coaster. Arcade games that appear to be real. Computer terminals that light up. The giant-size Doctor Deathstar, MacMillan's new Christmas toy, should have smoke and laser light and, says Wagner, "look like something you wouldn't want to pick up unless you're wearing gloves." Last, but decidedly not least, is something fabulous to get Josh back to boyhood. Think Cape Kennedy. Rockets. Smoke. "Mike wants a big effect here," summarizes Wagner. "A spectacular effect."

12:00 noon

Wagner is simultaneously in the early rounds of pruning his budget, an ongoing activity. Working with the Hudson Scenic shop representative, Corky Boyd, on one side and *Big* general manager, Robert Kamlot, on the other, Wagner agrees to trims that each knock out thousands of dollars. (He will do this again. And again.) Gone is Cynthia Benson's house—a savings of $27,750. A smaller school bathroom set—a savings of $13,000. They even shave a little on Wild Thunder.

"You're turning this into a show that can be done," says Boyd, admiringly. Kamlot nods: "That is the reason for this meeting."

Wednesday, April 5, 1995

4:00 pm

Writing session at Shire's Greenwich Village townhouse. Shire plays electric piano, his ears covered by headphones and his notes soundless, while Weidman is in the rocking chair, taking notes on his yellow legal pad. Maltby sits at the edge of the brown-and-white checkered sofa, totally detached from everything and everyone around him, tapping out lyrics on the laptop computer he's set up on the coffee table.

The three men work smoothly together. Yalies all, they dress alike in their jeans and crew-neck sweaters, and each leavens essential seriousness with considerable humor. Weidman, the youngest at 48, often prefaces his remarks with phrases like, "Just to make this more misery-inducing..."

Shire, 57, is a quiet, gray-haired man who almost always looks somber. Maltby, also 57, is talkative, usually smiling, seemingly unflappable, distracted. Shire is slim and Maltby portly and as the show nears Broadway, Maltby notes that while Shire is losing weight and he's gaining, as a team they weigh about the same.

Today they are working on a new first song for the second act. Sometimes Maltby looks up and sings out a lyric in perfect rap beat. "What you're listening to," Maltby says after one such outburst, "is two people who said they will never have rap music in this show finally coming to terms with the fact it's the language of 13-year-olds in the '90s."

The result: the show's funniest song and one which will go on to please audiences and critics alike. Lines like "I'm so pissed, I'm talking like a rapper" and "Nothing's worse crap than a little white Polish boy from Jersey talking rap" will literally stop the show, drawing applause from audience after audience. Brett Tabisel's performance as that little white Polish boy will help him garner "Best Supporting Actor" nominations for Tony and Drama Desk awards and win him a Theatre World award for an "outstanding debut" this season.

Today, however, the song is too new, too fragile for confidence. Besides, the writing is overshadowed by the back and forth wavering on postponement. Sometimes one of them brings up the subject, but more often it's producer Freydberg calling with yet another schedule, yet another possible city or two.

Everyone freezes each time the phone rings. Weidman, for instance, is worried about how postponement could affect his work with Sondheim on their new show; it could (and will) wind up having to be postponed. Right now, he's finding it tough to work amid so much indecision. "I only *seem* calm," he says. "It makes me want to remain immobile until the ride stops."

4:30 pm

Ockrent arrives. "It has to do with guarantees and money," he explains. "Boston represents a quagmire. It's a money pit.

It seems to me there isn't much chance of staying on this schedule unless they're willing to stomach the risk of losing a fortune in Boston."

They aren't. When the group calls Freydberg a while later on the speaker phone to complain about a possible logo—"It sucks," they roar in unison—the producer launches into a rage. "We are in a catch-22," he shouts. "We have a show that is written and designed too big for any theater we can go into. There is no way to do this show. It is unproducible. It belongs in a 15,000 seat theater."

It is so big, he says several times, he doesn't even want to produce it. Give it to some other producer, he hollers. "Find a maniac and let him have it."

Calming down, he offers two alternatives: They can trim and go into New York cold in a couple months, or they can take it to Detroit in February. They would have guarantees in Detroit they can't get in Boston. Either way, he says, "the operative word is 'cut.'"

Ockrent argues that its running costs are less than those of *Crazy for You*. Freydberg counters that they will be much more later. The conversation ends inconclusively, and everyone looks depressed.

"You just don't know with a new show until it's done," Ockrent says. "And that's why there are so many revivals."

Thursday, April 6, 1995
11:00 am

Ockrent is trying to maintain what he calls "a sense of reality." It isn't easy.

"Reality is quite scary," Ockrent explains. "The producers could lose $10 million in one fell swoop, and we're all liable to lose 1½ years of our lives doing something that can close in three days. It's no wonder the pressure is so extreme."

Contemporary shows present additional problems. "*Damn Yankees*, *Pajama Game* and *West Side Story* were all set in their own time, but there have been very few for good reason. We tend to regard our own present day as rather boring. It doesn't lend itself to pastiche. It is only looking back that we

29

find symbols and romance; we're just coming to a time when we're romanticizing the '60s.

"We know what we wear now, and it doesn't lend itself to romanticism. People who come to see the show will have been to the Port Authority and F.A.O. Schwarz, so you're dealing with concrete things that have to be represented in a way that makes sense to people. You can't cheat on the emotions of your own time either."

Now he has this additional worry about postponement. "As a freelance director, you really juggle thoughts and ideas and get excited about things on an ad hoc, almost haphazard, basis—a bit here and a bit there. You see what crystallizes out and gets some momentum. I have several shows in various states of preparation; you absolutely have to. If I didn't, when this was over, it would be another 14 months or two years before I could do another show. It would be financially impossible.

"If a show gets postponed like this, suddenly the whole schedule of work is thrown into chaos."

12:30 pm

Meeting at Serino Coyne ad agency. Lobby walls are covered with posters for *Les Misérables*, *Cats*, *Miss Saigon*, and other shows. *Big* producers, ad execs and publicists are in the boardroom talking logos when Ockrent arrives, and the dance-on piano keyboard that will torment them onstage is already an issue.

Agency chairman Nancy Coyne reports a key focus group finding: everyone who saw the film has fond memories of Hanks and Loggia dancing on the floor piano. As a result, all logo finalists incorporate a keyboard and dancing feet.

Objection from Ockrent: "This moment in the show occurs about three scenes in. If you focus on this one moment, and it's over in the first 20 minutes, you've seen the show."

Objection overruled. Circus impresario Feld asks, "What is the purpose of this?" then answers, "To sell tickets. We want to create an identity. I don't want to have to write a book to explain what we're selling. We've got to do it in the simplest

possible way. There is an expectation that somewhere in this show will be the piano scene."

Feld pauses dramatically, then continues. "I made the greatest mistake of my career about three years ago. After 20 years of putting the circus together, I was sick of the flying trapeze. Take it out, I said. I got hate mail, so I put it back in. When people left the circus, they didn't talk about it. But it was the *expectation* going in. There can be 35 scenes better than this in the show. It doesn't matter. But to get them in there, you have to grab them with a hook."

Freydberg agrees: "You want to remind people that this is the musical of *that* film, because there is this big mass audience out there that doesn't go to theater. The same one that goes to see *Beauty and the Beast* and sits up there in the second balcony. Any theatergoer knows you don't buy the second balcony. But that's the audience we're after, and in our case, it's make or break. *Beauty and the Beast* was the first show many of them went to, and *Big* could be the second."

Friday, April 7, 1995

Ockrent reports that script changes are almost at a dead halt because of the stalemate on postponement. "We're in a generally chaotic state," he confesses. "But even if we appear to be on calmer seas today, and come out of it all smiley and hugging and kissing each other, it does not mean that we won't enter choppy waters again."

Wednesday, April 12, 1995

Creative team meets with Freydberg over breakfast to talk options. One possiblilty is following the *Show Boat* route and starting in Toronto, then reassembling another company as replacements and heading to New York in fall, 1996. The advantage is they'd have four or five months to learn the show and build up word of mouth; they could arrive on Broadway at the start of the season rather than the end. If they do it the other way, with Detroit in February and a spring opening, they could be too dependent on Tony nominations.

When he and Freydberg looked at the numbers, says Feld, "I said, 'This is crazy. We're rushing, we're not ready and we're

going to lose $1.5 million in Boston the way this is set up. Let's wait. Let's not go forward until we feel really comfortable. There's too much at stake.' In five years, nobody is going to know if you're six months late, if you have a hit."

Monday, April 17, 1995

Press release announces *Big* will now open in spring, 1996, at the Shubert Theatre. Freydberg is quoted saying *Crazy for You* was expected to run until at least the end of 1995 and noting commitments of Stroman and Ockrent to *A Christmas Carol*.

Tuesday, May 2, 1995

Maltby and Shire do presentation at Freydberg office for Toronto theater operator David Mirvish.

Wednesday, May 10, 1995

Maltby and Shire do presentation at Freydberg office for Detroit theater operator Joseph Nederlander.

Tuesday, May 16, 1995, Los Angeles

Freydberg's back on the Coast, and his mood is much better. Finally, the indecision is over. He was talking to theater owners in both Toronto and Detroit so seriously, he says, that he began to worry it was like dating two women at the same time—both would get fed up and leave.

When the producer couldn't get assurances that the Toronto theater would be available, he says, he essentially went into a meeting with Nederlander knowing Detroit was his only choice. But he seems pleased with the outcome: the Nederlanders have a six-show subscription season, and *Big* could wind up slotted between *Joseph and the Amazing Technicolor Dreamcoat* and *Beauty and the Beast*. (It does, in fact.) "Those are perfect shows to coincide with ours. One of the reasons I wanted to go to Detroit so badly is that *Beauty and the Beast* is on their subscription. If they get that family audience, that same audience would come to us."

Various tie-ins with F.A.O. Schwarz, the upscale toy re-

32

tailer, also look promising, adds Freydberg. "Every time you say F.A.O. Schwarz, it will remind people of that film," he says, "which is good and bad. It's bad because you have to make sure that moment works. What's good is that it identifies the show. And there will be a lot of articles about a major corporation coming in and participating in the producing."

Which, he will see, is also both good and bad.

Wednesday, June 7, 1995

John Eyler had been president and chief executive officer of F.A.O. Schwarz for just two years when Freydberg first approached him about *Big*. Freydberg was impressed in 1993 with FAO's extensive store displays for the film, *Jurassic Park*, and had a hunch something like that could work for theater. With *Big*, the producer had his chance; Eyler and FAO could not have been more receptive.

The *Big* video is consistently one of the store's top 10 sellers, and toy pianos modeled on the piano that figured so prominently in the film are among the store's most popular items, particularly at Christmas. The piano scene has actually become "sort of a signature for our company," says Eyler, an amiable Northwesterner. "This company is 133 years old and probably remembered by more people for that scene from a movie than for any other occurrence in its 133-year history."

Besides agreeing to provide props and toy store design expertise, Eyler was open to redesigning their already successful dance-on keyboards and developing new products with Feld's marketing people. F.A.O. Schwarz could sell tickets in the Fifth Avenue store and host the opening night party there.

"We're retailers, not theater people, but we are also show people," says Eyler. "Our stores are creations of fantasy. If ever it would make sense, this would be it. Several of us went to the [March] reading, and our conclusion, understanding fully who the players would be in different disciplines, was very enthusiastic about its chances for success."

Eyler himself was clearly thrilled: "The best day I ever had in retailing, and I've been in it 24 years, was the first Christmas season I was here. The day after Thanksgiving, we

opened our doors, and the lines were down Fifth Avenue. There was a half-hour wait to get in the store, it was cold, people had snow on their shoulders and every single person who came through the revolving door broke into a smile. The reason that *Big* is special from our point of view is that spiritually it's very much like we are. It's a joyful film. It is hard to watch *Big* the movie and, I believe, *Big* the musical, and not have a smile on your face and be transformed. Therein lies a special bond between us and that property."

Friday, June 9, 1995

Rehearsals are underway for the show's fourth and final reading, set for Saturday.

Jenkins takes a break from rehearsals, and his manner is friendly, animated, sort of kid-like. He has short, curly brown hair, blue eyes, and an ingenuousness that reinforces rather than discourages his resemblance to Tom Hanks.

Much as Hanks' performance haunts the show, so did it haunt its casting. Not only is Hanks an even bigger star today than he was in 1988, but it remains one of his signature roles; this very year he recreated the keyboard scene onstage at Harvard when he accepted a Hasty Pudding Award.

(Actually, Hanks wasn't even the first choice for the film. Harrison Ford had been attached to the property before director Penny Marshall came in. Marshall had first wanted Robert DeNiro, and Mark confirms that Hanks was essentially a compromise. Twentieth Century Fox and producer James Brooks were then willing to wait for Hanks to finish another project, even though it meant opening after three other movies with similar themes.)

Casting wish lists included such prominent actors as Robert Downey, Jr., and Scott Bakula, and a few well-known actors did audition. Ockrent theorized that *Crazy for You*, even with Gershwin music, could have sold more tickets faster with stars, and everyone involved observed the sales impact Glenn Close had on *Sunset Boulevard*.

Some well-known performers were busy with television or film work. When others were interested, their agents

often advised against a commitment that could last a year or more. As casting director Vinnie Liff also points out, "The movie is too fresh in our memories. I think that's a reason why certain stars were gun-shy. They asked, 'How are we going to be able to eradicate that incredible performance?'"

Jenkins will be questioned again and again about recreating a role immortalized by the much-loved Hanks, but he says, "Honestly, it's not in my mind when I'm working on it." The comparison, he feels, would only be a problem if he hadn't thought much of Hanks' performance. "Since I loved the movie and his performance, it's a rather warm shadow to be standing in."

Saturday, June 10, 1995

Final reading. Six of the songs are so new that Shire characterizes them as "dripping placenta." After guests leave, the creative team reviews what it just saw, scene by scene, actor by actor. Ockrent and Stroman are cool on the new farewell duet, which means more songwriting, and script problems persist. Susan Lawrence still has to be transformed into someone warmer and more likeable, and the catalyst still has to be a magical, special Josh Baskin.

Both film and musical have similar beginnings, but the adult Josh fares a bit differently onstage. The show descends into what Ockrent later calls "plot hell," the first act conclusion that will plague them through Detroit. Josh and MacMillan meet at F.A.O. Schwarz, the toy executive offers his new, child-like friend a job, and Josh reports to the office. World-weary junior executive Susan appears, is dispatched by evil Paul to Josh's loft ("the loft scene") to spy on him but becomes charmed instead. (The means of enchantment will later change from the inflatable Magic Castle to the Official Startraveller's Compass Ring.) She spends the night—chastely—and they meet again at the office party. Something happens. End of act.

The second act begins with kids singing *about* the mall, Mrs. Baskin singing *in* the mall, Josh having a nightmare *at*

the mall. (The mall set was expensive.) Back at the office Josh and Susan start talking work and end up in bed. His jubilant morning after results in a toy based on the Zoltar machine, after which Susan takes him to meet her friends at their East Side apartment ("the yuppie scene"). He realizes he's in over his head, wants to go home, finds a Zoltar machine in a warehouse. Something else happens. End of show.

About one-third of the show is constantly being rewritten, and that third is scattered throughout the show from the middle of the first act onward. Neither act has a satisfactory ending at this point, and everyone knows it.

But many of the performances today were quite good, and they decide to hire several of the actors. They are still hoping to land a star for MacMillan and will soon audition kids. Well aware of the voice and height changes that accompany puberty, they are waiting as long as possible before casting the pivotal roles of young Josh and his friend Billy. "We'll be casting 12-year-old boys every six months for the rest of our lives," sighs Shire. Ockrent rolls his eyes: "We should be so lucky."

Two days after the reading, Ockrent heads off to London to direct a play for the Royal Shakespeare Company. Weidman goes back to the musical he is writing with Sondheim, and Stroman starts preparing for a fall workshop of John Kander and Fred Ebb's new show, *Steel Pier*. Shire and his family take off for the Cape Cod house they'd rented when the show was set for a summer tryout in Boston.

Thursday, June 22, 1995

Wagner continues cutting his budget. Freydberg says the first set bids came in at $2.8 million (and will eventually be slashed to $1.5 million). This is, after all, the same team that sent all those dancers onto rooftops and automobiles in *Crazy for You*. As Wagner puts it, "You go for the moon and then start backing up."

It's a competitive market out there. Everyone involved with *Big*—including Wagner—says again and again that theirs is a simple story. But the Broadway patron, having paid as much as $70 for a ticket, is now accustomed to—and apparently

36

enthralled by—such props as descending chandeliers and ascending helicopters.

Production values have to be high when there's no star, Wagner explains, and that usually means expensive sets and crews. But the 1,449-seat Shubert Theatre has a second balcony. Since second balcony seats don't often sell well and high-priced seats are fewer, operating costs have to be held down.

Victor/Victoria, for instance, has both a huge star, Julie Andrews, and a theater heavily weighted toward expensive orchestra seats rather than cheaper balcony ones. *Big* has neither.

So Ockrent and Wagner keep whittling away at their original design. Wagner speaks of shows as ships, with directors as captains, and, he says, "The captain is always right. There has to be a single vision. If you can't make his vision come to life, the show won't work."

Wagner hadn't even seen the movie *Big* when he agreed to work on the show. "I had such a wonderful feeling for Stro and Mike, and knew the hurdles they had gone over on *Crazy for You*," he says. "This was at least a tested story."

He did eventually see the film, of course. Also inspired by architect Michael Graves' designer dollhouses, Wagner says he has tried "to look at this piece through the eyes of a 13-year-old. The impulse I keep having is to make things simple. Geometrical. Almost post-modern. I love the colors of the Michael Graves stuff—all strong pastels and no pure color. It's kind of a child's view of the world. They see shapes, not detail."

Friday, July 14, 1995, London

At their Kensington flat, as at their New York penthouse, Ockrent and Stroman work on the show.

The director and choreographer appear to have similar metabolisms. Propelled by nervous energy, they rarely sit still for very long, whether in conversation, at the rehearsal hall or during meetings. They also share a general good humor and, for some reason, both nearly always dress in black. (Stroman's work appearance is so predictable—a ponytail

pulled through a black hat, black shirt, legs covered in black tights and legwarmers—that William Ivey Long later dresses one dancer in *Big* that way, complete with Stroman's *Crazy for You* jacket.)

Choreography is taking shape now. They are developing an idea for a corps of teenagers whose behavior, expressed through movement, will reflect what Josh leaves behind when he becomes an adult. The teenagers begin as separate clumps of girls and boys who want nothing to do with each other, then later mix and mingle. At the end of the second act, they pair off, a courtship ritual the grown-up Josh will miss unless he heads back home to childhood.

Among current concerns are the "buttons"—or endings—of different songs. Ockrent likes to stage his theater pieces cinematically, and, says Stroman, he does so mainly with dance and movement.

"You used to black out, then wait for the scene to change," she says. "Now the collaboration of director, set designer and choreographer can make that seamless and more like a cinematic crossfade—something we did in *Crazy for You* and *Show Boat*. I feel audiences today really need that because they are more geared to cinematic stories that never stop. The number has to propel you right into the set change and next scene."

Dance music arranger David Krane joins them here for a week. Sometimes they work at the upright piano in the dining room, but, more often, they just talk things through. "Stro is able to visualize and construct things without having the bodies around," says Krane. "When she teaches something to her dancers, it seems like it has been performed somewhere. But it hasn't. It's been performed in her head."

Monday, July 31, 1995

John Eyler takes an overnight flight to Amsterdam to meet with senior executives of F.A.O. Schwarz' corporate parent, the Dutch conglomerate, Koninklijke Bijenkorf Beheer, about several FAO matters, including investments in *Big*. "We were a little bit unsure how to approach a publicly-owned parent company about investing in a Broadway show," admits Eyler.

"It wasn't something they receive requests for on a daily basis."

He needn't have worried. "They loved the concept," he says. "They told me that if I could negotiate an agreement that properly rewards the company if it's successful and secures F.A.O. Schwarz' visibility as a sponsor from a public relations point of view, they would be supportive of the investment."

Eyler catches the 1:30 p.m. flight back to New York and is home in time for dinner with his family.

Monday, August 21, 1995

Expectations are building. Writes Ken Mandelbaum in *Theater Week*'s musical theater season preview: "The delightful and touching movie about a 12-year-old boy who wishes himself into the body of a 30-year-old is a wonderful property for musicalization, and with songwriters—Richard Maltby, Jr. and David Shire—at the top of their field and very right for this material, *Big* seems to me the season's most promising new musical."

Friday, August 25, 1995

Stroman shops F.A.O. Schwarz for first time for dance props. She picks out such things as devil stick batons, oversized inflatable balls, boomerangs and paper planes. No charge, of course.

She, Wagner and their assistants will shop FAO on and off through Broadway previews. Props include many, many plush animal toys, some big, some small, to camouflage the floor piano. When Wagner needs an 8½ foot bear and all they have are smaller or bigger bears, Eyler calls FAO's supplier in Germany and has one custom-made. Later, worried that designers might need toys that could get sold at Christmas, he has likely goods pulled and set aside for them.

Friday, September 8, 1995

New York Times On Stage, and Off column leads with news that F.A.O. Schwarz will be a major investor in and co-producer of *Big*. Writer Peter Marks calls it "a match made in marketing heaven."

Monday, September 18, 1995

Stroman, Krane, assistant choreographer Ginger Thatcher and dance captain Stacey Todd Holt are in the rehearsal hall putting the summer's dance ideas on their feet.

The choreographer has augmented those ideas with frequent visits to both malls and record stores, watching kids interact and listening to their music. Her "straw dance," set at a mall in the second act, was inspired by teens making noises with their straws in paper cups, for instance. Her observation of how packs of kids do add-on steps, one starting and others following, and their ways of signalling one another also suggested the dances in *Big*.

She has tried not to be so contemporary that her dances seem dated a year from now. "If you did something totally hiphop, MTV, on-the-nose rap or Michael Jackson style, it would lose interest in a moment," she says. "So I had to come up with something new.

"There are elements of hiphop, but it's all based on the psyche of 13-year-olds. Because pure hiphop or pure break dancing is not theatrical, it had to become behavioral choreography. For example, there are steps the girls do where they are first tomboys, then young ladies, then Power Rangers, because at that age, it's not clear."

The choreographer's "dance pre-production" will continue another two weeks, break while she works on *A Christmas Carol* and finish up just before *Big* rehearsals start in December. It isn't an ideal plan but the only one she can handle with both shows underway.

They're using a keyboard mockup, some props and a few live kids. "The idea is to create with them many of the steps and get the shape of numbers," Krane explains. "Then we can rehearse with something very specific."

Monday, September 25, 1995

Dance pre-production continues. Stroman is staging the sequence that leads to Josh's first sexual experience. Susan has just sung about her own girlhood "Dancing All the Time," and when Josh joins her to dance, the relationship between

them changes. "I Want to Know," currently a duet sung by both young Josh and adult Josh, expresses some of the feelings a 13-year-old boy might have just then, when "what happens next scares me half to death."

Stroman is playing Susan, Holt is playing big Josh and Thatcher is playing little Josh. What they discover is that the song doesn't work onstage as a duet. "They were slow dancing and feeling the emotions one feels when falling in love, and the singing broke the focus," Stroman explains. "But if we kept the voice of the child and supported it visually [with the adult couple off to the side], it made that moment powerful."

"I Want to Know" becomes a solo for little Josh.

Thursday, October 12, 1995

Afternoon audition today for shy young Josh and wise-cracking pal Billy.

Most of these kids already have professional credits, not to mention agents. While none are hired on the spot, it is a very successful day. Seen for the first time are Graham Bowen and Brandon Espinoza, later selected for the ensemble and as understudies, plus Brett Tabisel, who will wind up playing Billy, and Patrick Levis, who will play little Josh.

Levis, from Silver Spring, Maryland, is among several boys whose families brought them in from out of town; some have come from as far away as Miami and Kansas City. The age range is 10 to 14, many are exactly 4'8" tall and at least half of them sing "Where Is Love?" from *Oliver!*

5:45 pm

Auditions end, and Ockrent is out the door. He charges down five flights of stairs, too much in a hurry to wait for the elevator, and grabs a cab uptown for another round of children's auditions, this time for *A Christmas Carol*. There, looking totally fresh, Ockrent makes notes on papers that rest on a thick black notebook marked, "*Big* script."

Friday, October 13, 1995

Adult audition today at Actors' Equity offices, where the

41

ladies room is labelled "Dolls" and the men's room, "Guys."
Seven lithe, attractive women are auditioning for the ensemble.

For maybe 10 minutes, Stroman and Thatcher show them
dance steps to "Coffee, Black," an upbeat production number, after which Stroman and Thatcher step aside and watch.
The women repeat the steps as a group. Then, two at a time,
they perform the sequence, swap places and do it again.

The dancers go off to change, then come back to sing. Focus shifts to conductor Gemignani, a bear-like figure who is
perhaps Broadway's most sought-after musical director.

Gemignani has an audition grading system he's developed
over the years to remind him later of someone he might not
otherwise recall. He's used the grading to audition Sondheim's
shows, and he's using it on *Big*. For example, Gemignani says
he gives a B- to a performer who can get by in the chorus but
not do solos. C+ to B- is a gray area, he adds; the actor needs
another attribute—like dancing well—before he says yes.

"A C+ means you can barely carry a tune," says Gemignani.
"You wouldn't get in the way but you wouldn't add anything.
Music-wise, a C+ is wasted space, but there may be other
reasons to hire that singer. If we all like somebody, it's our
job to figure out if we can make adjustments."

New shows are particularly difficult, Gemignani says. He
can be more flexible on *Crazy for You* now, he explains, because he knows the show, its traps and its pitfalls. But on a
new show, there are so many unknowns. "You have to cover
all the bases—music in the show today may not be there tomorrow. You've got to protect the show and yourself so you
have the tools to work with."

Saturday, October 14, 1995

Invited reading of *Steel Pier*, Kander and Ebb's new musical about marathon dancing. After a week of working both
Steel Pier and *Big*, Stroman narrates the three-hour *Steel
Pier* reading today, then will perform a similar task at
tomorrow's day-long production meeting on *Big*.

Stroman's involvement in *Steel Pier*, her most likely project
after *Big*, is an example of both the long gestation of shows
and the freelancer's continual speculation. One way that

freelancers offset risk is by saying yes to several shows, then hoping they don't all happen at the same time. Because *Big*'s postponement means Stroman, Ockrent, Gemignani and others are often working on *A Christmas Carol* simultaneously, auditions back up or get shunted to Sundays, and everyone looks exhausted most of the time.

Sunday, October 15, 1995

Full day production meeting. Standard practice for Ockrent, such gatherings bring crew and creative team together before technical rehearsals. "Look at them," Robert Kamlot says as maybe 40 people file in. "All these people are on our payroll, and the cast isn't even here."

Despite the wide range of disciplines, there is an odd homogeneity to the group. The drummer has a gray ponytail and a ring through his eyebrow, but many of the others look more like college professors and business executives than sound designers, costume assistants, electricians and magic consultants.

Weidman reads his script, the musical staff sings, dancers dance. Wagner and assistants wheel in a platform with a small stage and put on their travelling set show. Some scenes go quickly, some not. People with one sort of expertise help people with another; F.A.O. Schwarz executives make suggestions on props and producer Feld helps out on lighting. Discussion seems endless on how to pull off the keyboard dance number, a clear preview of horrors to come.

Gemignani says Ockrent did the same sort of thing on *Crazy for You*: "When I started that show, I knew everything about it. If something's wrong, he'll fix it, no matter what it takes."

Concludes Freydberg, who authorized today's $400 lunch tab and other bills: "What you're seeing is some very, very prepared people."

Monday, October 16, 1995

Having done well in the textile business, Ken Greenblatt has the money and time to indulge his passion for Broadway musicals. His Kenneth-John Productions shares an office suite

43

with Missbrenner fabric company, of which he is president, and the waiting room is strewn with issues of *Variety* along with garment industry trade papers. The entrance to Greenblatt's corner office is ringed with theatrical posters, and a xeroxed copy of the *Big* logo is taped to his office door.

Greenblatt grew up in New York and spent many childhood birthdays at the theater. His resume lists all 11 Broadway shows he's already co-produced—among them *La Cage aux Folles*, *Grand Hotel* and *Baby*—and talking about Tony awards, he spins around to pick one up and plop it on his desk.

He will be a frequent presence in Detroit, and afterwards, back in New York, he and his wife Sandi will move in from the suburbs temporarily so they can hang out at rehearsals. They contributed a photograph of their son, Shon, for MacMillan's office desk. In one scene set in a mall, three teenage girls flash Greenblatt's credit cards. (He thinks they've expired.)

Tossing off remarks like, "Susan Stroman is head and shoulders above Tommy Tune, and he's 6'6"," Greenblatt often says he can't imagine ever again finding a property that so enchants him.

"Every piece fits," Greenblatt says. "The square hole and the square peg, the round hole and round peg. I feel we have a Cal Ripken, Jr., in every position. And it was the easiest show to finance that I've ever been involved with."

Greenblatt says that he personally invested $500,000 as an example, and "If any of my investors want their money back, I'd be glad to write a check for the whole $5 million of my half."

Wednesday, October 18, 1995

Eyler also comes away from the production meeting impressed. He's been on the road opening six stores in five weeks, and found the day "surprisingly familiar. There is a very parallel process between bringing a store and a musical to life. You tap into all the strengths of your team—concepts, design, refinement, lighting, visual, mechanical—and on the targeted

day, you open the doors.

"There's not a single element that's weak. The score is wonderful; I came away humming the tunes and haven't even heard it orchestrated. Several of the ballads are quite moving, and you can just see what Susan Stroman's going to do. We love the theme, and we think the property has a timeless message. We believe this is going to be a smash hit."

Eyler has on his desk final agreements regarding F.A.O. Schwarz' participation in producing *Big*. He expects the five-page contract to be signed this week. (It will be signed October 28.) Nobody will confirm the exact size of the retailer's investment, said to be about $1 million.

As his rather austere and uncluttered office indicates, Eyler is also a businessman, not just a toymaker. "Most people I know in retailing are used to ups and downs in business. You don't get too excited when something is financially successful, and you don't get too depressed when something isn't financially successful. It's just part of the game. The secret is to win more than you lose.

"Are we tremendously optimistic and excited? Yes. Is there a risk that we're so caught up in the enthusiasm that we're not realistic that, for whatever reason, the public will possibly not embrace this show? Of course. That's a possibility. But it will be very disappointing."

Thursday, October 19, 1995

Busker Alley, the new Tommy Tune musical, will not start a Broadway run tonight.

The show had stopped at several cities en route to New York, including Costa Mesa, California. At the conclusion of the show's performance on June 27 at the Orange County Performing Arts Center, Tune told his audience: "If you like the show, tell your friends. If not, tell them you saw *Cats*."

Tune and company continued their pre-Broadway tour until earlier this month, when the dancer/director broke his foot performing at the Tampa Bay Performing Arts Center in Florida. The show was scheduled to begin Broadway previews tonight and open on November 16.

Is it possible *Victor/Victoria* will be the only other new musical this season?

Wednesday, October 25, 1995

Victor/Victoria opens on Broadway. Reviews aren't great, but box office certainly is. And stays that way.

Sunday, November 5, 1995

Open casting call for kids' ensemble is set for 10:00 a.m. at Joan of Arc High School. More than 100 boys and girls are waiting by 8:30, and by day's end, 511 show up.

Some are sent home because they're the wrong age or size, while others head to the gym for dancing eliminations. Stroman and staff teach a series of steps, watch groups of 30 or 40 perform them, then continue to cut the groups down. Weidman finds it interesting that the girls applaud as each group finishes, but the boys don't.

Among those later selected are Spencer Liff, whose family flew in from Southern California, and Enrico Rodriguez from suburban Detroit. Lori Aine Bennett, Samantha Robyn Lee, and Lizzy Mack, the trio of girls who will open the show, are all discovered today.

Ockrent later tells WOR-TV: "All the kids who are now in the show just popped out at us."

Tuesday, November 7, 1995

MacMillan is finally cast. The toy company executive will be played by Jon Cypher, the veteran stage and TV actor who had auditioned last February with a bad knee.

Everyone wanted a well-known, "audience friendly" MacMillan, and an endless parade of prominent actors had passed through 890 Broadway in recent weeks. The likely commitment of a year lost them such potential players as Charles Durning and Ed Asner, says casting director Vinnie Liff. "John Cullum was going into *Show Boat* on Broadway, and Ned Beatty was going into the Vancouver/L.A. company," Liff continues. "For other actors, it came down to the dollars and cents for such a long time. Jon is being well paid, but

there were certain agents who quoted monies I said would be impossible to pay for that role."

Now silver-haired and 63, Cypher had played Prince Charming in Rodgers and Hammerstein's TV musical *Cinderella* opposite Julie Andrews in 1957. He understudied Richard Kiley in *Man of La Mancha* and appeared on Broadway in 10 other shows as well. But that was 25 years ago, and although he's starred in assorted musicals in Los Angeles and elsewhere, the actor's current celebrity comes primarily from his seven seasons as quirky Police Chief Fletcher P. Daniels on *Hill Street Blues.*

Enter fate. Cypher had broken his right knee in 1992 during a dress rehearsal as Fagin in *Oliver!* in Pittsburgh. Then, two weeks after his Los Angeles audition for *Big* last February, he broke the knee again in an auto accident. Surgery corrected it, and, he says, "It was the most amazingly serendipitous thing that ever happened to me."

Actually, confides Cypher, "I asked God to give it to me... I was in New York filming *Law and Order* a year ago when *Sunset Boulevard* was opening. George Hearn is a close friend, and I wanted to leave an opening night note for him. I couldn't even get close because of the crowds, until finally one of the guards recognized me. I dropped off my note, walked up 46th St. and said, 'God, give me one more shot.'"

Tuesday, November 14, 1995

Sale closes today on the Shire/Conn home in Sherman Oaks. They had planned to relocate to New York after *Big* opened but decided not to wait. They sold the place in the Village as well and moved out beyond Manhattan to Snedens Landing. "David and I grew up dreaming about theater, not film," says Conn. "We wanted to be where our dreams were."

Meanwhile, Maltby and Shire still have no duet between Josh and Susan for the end of the show. The writers want a reprise, but there's no song—at this point—that they want to reprise. "You need an emotional statement from Josh that makes you realize why you just spent two hours watching his progress," says Shire. "Thirteen-year-olds don't make philo-

sophical statements, but we need to find something that Josh can say that's a terrific lyric for a song and that Susan can sing with him later."

But there's still time. "This show won't get frozen until a couple days before it opens in New York," continues Shire. "Even during rehearsal, once the cast starts doing it, we'll see things not so apparent when we were at the table."

Sunday, November 19, 1995, Burbank, California

Open call children's auditions this weekend in Southern California, to be followed by more in Chicago. Total number auditioned so far for the 11 kids' parts: about 800.

"Because this is a new show, nothing is set," says Johnson-Liff's Ron LaRosa, a casting director who specializes in children. "We're waiting for Josh and Billy to walk in the door. We don't have a strict height limit or weight limit or voice quality yet. Once the mold has been set, it will be more about who can replace *these* kids. But right now, our minds are open.

"We're also not only looking for roles we haven't filled yet, but, because we expect this to be a hit, we look for replacements. When kids get too old or their voices change or they don't want to do it any longer, I've got to have a backlog of kids ready to go into the show who have been approved by everybody."

Californians Kari Pickler, 13, from Santa Ana and Joseph Medeiros, 11, from Modesto are both later selected as "swings" to stand-by for the children's ensemble. Medeiros sings Irving Berlin's "Stepping Out with My Baby" so well they teach him little Josh's song, "I Want to Know." He is also small and, given his age and height, he could play the show a long time.

Weidman is representing the creative team. "I tried to get out of it," he shrugs. "But Mike and Susan are in rehearsals for *A Christmas Carol*. David and Richard have more writing work than I do. That left me. If I stepped aside, there was nobody behind me to take my place."

Besides, it's a challenge. One boy looks like the roguish Billy but performs as the shy Josh, and Weidman tries directing him. The playwright carefully explains who the character is and how he behaves: "Think of Billy as an operator." The

boy listens, nods, then gives exactly the same performance.

Tuesday, November 28, 1995

There are meetings every day now of one kind or another, often at Wagner's studio. This morning there are people in about props, about lighting, about special effects.

The end of the first act is now set at Tavern on the Green—a lot of office parties take place there, Wagner says—and the restaurant helped designers with outdoor furniture and fabric samples for their outdoor lanterns. The resulting set, which will later host a big dance production number, also uses a lot of simple, cheap Christmas lights.

Ockrent calls Wagner all the time, day or night. "Mike's a good sailor, always ready for change," says Wagner. "You never know which direction the tempest is coming from or which way the wind is blowing. You have to be on your toes, always in touch with all the elements. And that's the way Mike works. He's always balancing everything.

"There are 1,000 moving parts. And just when you think you're on top of it, some part blows out and you have to rebuild it. It's like a bubbling soup and you try to dance on it. But you never know when it's going to boil over. And everybody's hungry."

Wednesday, December 6, 1995

Joseph Medeiros and his father fly in from Modesto, California. Joseph sings, dances and otherwise auditions for maybe half an hour, after which they go out to wait in the hallway for 20 minutes. Casting director Vinnie Liff comes down the hall toward them, puts out his hand and says, "Welcome to Broadway."

Medeiros is the last person cast for the show.

PART TWO: REHEARSALS

"Peter Brook once asked John Gielgud to tell the other actors something frightening. His response was, 'We open next week.'"

—Mike Ockrent, director,
January 24, 1996

For seven weeks starting December 11, *Big* takes over much of the fourth floor at 890 Broadway. One studio is set aside for rehearsing songs and scenes, another for dancing, another to gather costumes. Tailors and wigmakers operate out of small rooms up and down the hall.

Ockrent rehearsed *Me and My Girl*, *Crazy for You* and *A Christmas Carol* here, and many of his cast and crew worked on one or more of those shows. Sometimes they are still working on them: Gemignani attends *Big* rehearsals, then heads over to Madison Square Garden to conduct *A Christmas Carol*, and Holt is rehearsing *Big* while on call as a "swing" dancer for *Crazy for You* 25 blocks uptown.

The director usually uses the large studio, the one adjacent to the production office, for plotting scenes, reviewing music and directing ensemble sequences. The room itself is immense, with mirrors along one wall, windows along another. There, in sweats and tennis shoes, bottles of Evian water and tape recorders handy, actors learn and relearn lines and lyrics with assorted members of the creative and technical teams.

An outline of Detroit's Fisher Theatre stage is marked on the floor, where different colored tapes signify chunks of the set. F.A.O. Schwarz toys fill huge prop bins.

Many things happen at once during this time. Costumers photograph the cast, assembling head shots for wigs, body shots for costumes. The London-based wigmaker flies in to measure heads, and tailors take down arm, leg and other measurements. There are upwards of 220 costumes in the show and more than 70 wigs. The high numbers reflect the extensive ensemble work in the show, where each actor can play six or more different parts.

Many costumes will be "made"—constructed from scratch—at Barbara Matera design studios upstairs. Robin Wagner, costume designer William Ivey Long and their staffs seem constantly to be trudging up and down the stairs. So

do cast members en route to fittings and, in many cases, to math and science classes in the 6th floor schoolroom.

Monday, December 11, 1995

First day of rehearsal. Production assistants arrive by 9:15 a.m. They line up rows of chairs to face the tables where the creative team will be. They arrange boxes of scripts. They sharpen 60 pencils.

Actors, writers, producers and support staff start drifting in. Most know each other personally from prior Ockrent shows or from *Big*'s many readings, others by reputation. They hug, they kiss, they reminisce. Drummer Paul Pizzuti shows pictures of his nine-day-old daughter. Stroman confesses "frock shock": "It was like the first day of school. I didn't know what to put on." (Her choice is the black jeans, sweater and cap she nearly always wears.)

All day long there are previews of the future, from behavior patterns to work styles. The extroverts and introverts identify themselves. So do the stern producer and the ebullient producer, the people who will push themselves and the ones who will just get by. And when Ockrent starts the day by welcoming everyone to "a big adventure," he isn't kidding.

First preview: Scripts are distributed, after which 11 new script pages are distributed.

The actors read and sing through the script. Often they applaud one another—Jenkins' singing of the poignant "I Want to Go Home," Walsh's performance of the show's most likely hit, "Stop, Time." The kids, who are sitting together up front, laugh at all the dirty words. They enjoy the vomit scenes especially.

Second preview: It takes nearly two hours to get through the first act.

2:30 pm

Ockrent and Wagner walk everyone through a model of the set, narrating scene changes from the neighborhood to the carnival, the Port Authority bus terminal to F.A.O. Schwarz. Wagner and his staff drop hanging sets in from above their

small stage and move three-sided on-stage pieces in and out of place with great ease.

Ockrent personalizes the little set for his audience, telling individual actors where they will stand, which houses they will inhabit. The boss' secretary stands here. The nasty boyfriend works there. The big keyboard production number will look like this.

What he can't tell them (because he doesn't know yet) is what a nightmare all those moving parts will be when they get to Detroit. The three-sided units, each 14 feet tall and weighing maybe half a ton, will move along tracks that can be jammed with something as small as a ballpoint pen. The piano keyboard will be in chunks so heavy that each will require three men to lift it. And the stuff that will drop in from above will be stacked and released by a complex computer program that doesn't adapt well to the unexpected.

William Ivey Long is on next. He drags out huge boards, some of them taller than he is, which are covered with photographs of New York-area suburbanites, commuters and shoppers. Even the kids in his photos don't look particularly stageworthy.

So Long will employ "heightened realism," and one storytelling device is color. At the show's start, girls will be in yellow, boys in blue, and yellows don't talk to blues. When the two sexes start to mingle at the mall, they will wear clothes whose colors work well together. He's thinking rainbow pastels for when they start to mate toward the end of the show. Billy, whom he describes as the show's "active verb," will stand out in red.

Shire is brief. He explains how the hardest language to find has been the musical language of kids. His older son, Matthew, 20, managed a rock band part-time and took him to Tower Records at one point. Matthew was also once 13, "and I lived through knowing 13-year-olds are not the most expressive."

Maltby is even more brief. The lyricist warns everyone: "Pay no attention to the look on my face. I have some thought on my mind. It isn't you."

Possibly, he's thinking about the story which, after all, is what Weidman says captured all of their imaginations in the first place. "The story has great strengths to be told on a musical theater stage," Weidman says. "It's simple but has real depth and real meaning. It is filled with real warnings and wisdoms about the way we should live our lives."

That is the day's message: this is *serious* stuff. Ockrent even hands out six pages of "distilled wisdom" from Erik Erikson, Jean Piaget and others. His favorite is a quote from Schiller: "Man is perfectly human only when he plays."

Summarizes Ockrent: "We're dealing with kids who are on the cusp. The whole show is about that. If you miss out on that period, there are problems, and Josh finally sees that. Adults learn to see the world as it is, but kids see the world as they wish it to be. The sadness of growing up is learning this, and that's the essence of this show."

5:00 pm

Producers, advertising executives, publicists and technical people have gone now, and the actors move down the hall to the dance studio. Krane is at the piano as Stroman and her assistants run the cast through an assortment of steps, figuring out who does what best.

"I do this to see how far I can push some of the character people," says Stroman. "No one actually is a dancer. They're movers. Although I auditioned all of them, I need to see them once more to help me place them in the dance numbers."

Ockrent stops by. He can't contain his enthusiasm, chatting with his assistant, his stage manager, a visitor. The director points to one of the smaller boys. "He's just 11," Ockrent says. "He could play the show for a year."

Tuesday, December 12, 1995

Today, as every day, several things are going on at once, sometimes in separate rooms, sometimes all in the same room.

The largest rehearsal studio is starting to house props, big and small. There are mock-ups of the dance-on keyboard,

a sofa, a bunk bed. Cardboard boxes on tables off to the side are each marked by scene, then filled with appropriate items: caviar tins and wine bottle for one scene, clipboards and pens for another. A production assistant is pumping air into huge red balloons.

Upstairs, Robin Wagner is going over his budget numbers again. He slashed $1,000 off Josh's bunk bed, he says, by simplifying it. ("I said, 'Tell me how to make it cheaper? Wood instead of metal? Natural wood instead of painted wood?'") He also bought a mattress instead of having it made, then did the same with the kitchen cabinet and sink for Josh's house. The kitchen items would cost $2,795 to build, he says, and $795 at Home Depot. "It sounds silly," he admits, "but that's the way it works."

12:00 noon

Dan Jenkins is sitting with Ockrent at the side of the rehearsal room, their chairs very close together so they hear one another despite the ensemble singing maybe four yards away. Jenkins is eating a banana.

Josh is a 13-year-old, Ockrent reminds his star: "Josh feels he's been a fraud and believed his own fantasy. He has to be honest and truthful; he was an honest kid. The relationship with Susan can't exist. He has to go back. It's unsustainable. And *you* have to believe that."

Don't forget posture, the director warns. As an adult, Josh tries to stand very straight, which looks artificial. To illustrate his point, Ockrent lies face down on a nearby small table; he hangs over it, awkward and dangling, the way a pre-adolescent would.

3:00 pm

Crista Moore is now in the chair facing Ockrent. He wants Susan Lawrence to be tough at the beginning. Hard-boiled. Unsympathetic. She doesn't become vulnerable until she gets to Josh's loft and undergoes radical change.

Moore is immediately defensive. She doesn't want to create "a one-dimensional office ice queen." Susan should not be "a cliché." Susan should be more "human."

57

Ockrent smiles and keeps talking—slowly, carefully, pa-tiently. He and Moore have now initiated their director/actor tango, negotiating and clarifying their positions, and it is a dance that will become very familiar to them both as the show moves toward Broadway.

Susan is a woman who works in a toy company and has lost her ability to play, the director says. Josh helps her find it again. "She's not a woman in transition," Ockrent explains. "She's complacent, and she's a mess—she can't breathe, she smokes. She's saved by Josh. It's as if he waves a magic wand over her. That's what I feel we should be going for."

Moore looks more relaxed, easing back in her chair. "A bigger arc," she says, nodding. "I see. I'm totally in sync with who she is now."

Thursday, December 14, 1995

Ockrent tells, with some amusement, his dream of the night before: "Jim Freydberg told me that we were not doing the show. We had to do *Twelfth Night* instead, and Jim had already started it for me. With choirs. At 4 a.m., the whole audience was there, and a child stepped forward and looked at me and asked, 'What do we do now?' I woke up in a cold sweat."

The director is still chuckling as he starts moving actors into position. For the carnival scene, one ticket-taker sells tick-ets and gives refunds, he says, and the other gives kids a height test. "It's a very simple idea, and you guys just work it out to perfection." But should they need guidance, his experience with people like that is they're very morose. Actor Frank Vlastnik immediately looks morose.

Ockrent moves on. Production stage manager Steven Zweigbaum stands still, his stopwatch in his right hand. "The watch," he says, "is to find out if they *really* do have time to get around the stage the way Mike thinks they will. He moves on to the next thing, and I check to make sure the last thing worked okay."

Ockrent is a man in a hurry. Weidman tells a story, for

instance, about his friend Lynn Ahrens, who wrote the lyrics for *A Christmas Carol*. One day during rehearsal, Ockrent told Ahrens that he needed several lines of new lyrics. She said, "OK," and Ockrent went off to talk with conductor Gemignani about something. Five minutes later he returned and said, "Lynn, you have it yet?"

Now it's Weidman's turn. Ockrent needs dialogue, and calls out, "John, can you give me half a dozen lines of kids' chatter?" Then he turns back to the kids he's directing and says, "John will have them in a minute." The writer first looks stunned, then recovers and says, "Have you done your homework yet?"

Five lines to go.

Friday, December 15, 1995

Rehearsal and production staff are adjusting to a cast that is one-third adolescents and does things like sing "99 Bottles of Beer on the Wall" during breaks. Jenkins refers to them as his on-site research center: "Everything happening to them is happening to Josh. It couldn't be any handier."

Classes are in session most days on the 6th floor, where music from rehearsal trickles in through an open window. Each child is supposed to have at least three hours of school a day, and the number of students present at any given time varies, depending on who is needed where for which rehearsal.

Stroman is rehearsing the girl dancers downstairs, so today's class is just boys. Enrico Rodriguez, 15, is reading *Lord of the Flies*. Spencer Liff, 10, is identifying different kinds of matter. Brandon Espinoza, 13, is learning Spanish, and Brett Tabisel, also 13, is writing a paper on Abraham Lincoln.

When the young people aren't in class, they're largely the responsibility of their on-site "guardian," Robert Wilson. Earlier this week he met with nine stage moms and a dad, advising them to buy such necessities as oversized robes to protect costumes during meal breaks, and warning them that child actors get disappointed when their lines change and feel bad if they aren't chosen for publicity shots. Wilson, who has herded kids through Broadway and touring shows since '89,

says they may also need help dealing with costumes, wigs or haircuts they loathe.

He and teacher Eleanor Scott, who refer to themselves as "the Siegfried and Roy of child care," will accompany the cast to Detroit, then be on hand through the Broadway opening. Wilson may toss off lines like, "I better run upstairs now and see if any of the kids are on fire," but he is also the person backstage who gets out-of-town parents on the phone near a loudspeaker when their child is onstage. He used to be a stage manager, he says, and "This suits me. I'm very organized and silly at the same time and that's what we ask of these kids."

Wilson says that children "have a very short shelf life in this business," and it's particularly true on *Big*. Contracts have provisions for four-weeks' notice if the kids grow two or more inches, gain 10 or more pounds, or no longer can sing their roles because their voices change.

4:00 pm

School ends, and rehearsals continue on the New York Port Authority dance number. Gemignani figures he's "spent more time on this number than I spent in the Port Authority in my whole life."

Stroman uses—and reuses—the ensemble as three waves of travellers: commuters, tourists, and a group from Florida. A big hunk of bus comes across the stage, and they emerge from behind it to be greeted by belching bum John Sloman. (When Stroman said she needed some "wild noise" for the scene, Sloman volunteered his belch, which he can produce on cue.)

The choreographer gives each "clump" of bus passengers a departure point—one is coming in from Milburn, New Jersey, for instance—and each bus rider a history. She seems to be thinking as fast as she's speaking: "Frank is 85, with a cane. Clint is a 45-year-old businessman with a briefcase. Jill and Alex are on a date. They are 23. Joan is a cop—she needs a nightstick. John is a 55-year-old exhausted businessman with a spreadsheet and pencils. Jan plays a man and is a tuba player—she has a tuba case."

Stroman pauses for breath. "How old is she?" interjects Thatcher, who is writing it all down. Stroman replies: "Whatever age is fine."

The number, finally perfected days later, will be a shadow of its former self on Broadway. Within a few weeks, the song, "Like A Grown-Up," has been cut and the travellers are down to one group, not three. By the time *Big* leaves Detroit, the entire bus is gone and they disembark offstage. Sloman's still a bum, but not a belching one. Explains Ockrent: "It was a belch too far."

Saturday, December 16, 1995

Stroman works with the full cast for the first time today on "Fun," the piano keyboard number set at F.A.O. Schwarz. As work on this number stretches into days here, in Detroit and on Broadway, "Fun" quickly becomes a misnomer.

The film's two-minute piano scene will eventually stretch to nine minutes onstage and be choreographed again and again. What began with screenwriters Ross and Spielberg as a piano duet will be reconceived onstage with the scale of a Mahler symphony. Much as the filmmakers commissioned their dance-on piano after seeing a smaller one at FAO, so has the musical team commissioned one double the size of the film's.

Cast members have been using the rehearsal model, pushed off to the sides of the room until today, as a place to sit, eat lunch, drop backpacks. It is in chunks which, when assembled, will stretch across the entire stage, encompass four octaves and engage nearly the entire cast. Each chunk of that onstage keyboard will weigh 362 pounds, and the entire "instrument," with its multi-colored lights keyed to musical notes, will cost upwards of $100,000.

Stroman, who has always been aware of the expectations riding on this number, emphasizes the positive. "As a major plot point in terms of character development, it works very well," Stroman asserts. "They get together on a toy, something they both love, and they can play countermelody. That takes it to another dimension, about bonding harmoniously."

To hide the keyboard onstage, she and Wagner came up with a shelf covered by plush toys. Josh jumps on the shelf, it makes a sound, and he pushes the toys aside to reveal the piano. "It comes out of a child's surprise," Stroman says. "That wonderful time when a child plays with a jack-in-the-box and jack jumps out of the box. Then we developed a story, which involves a Pied Piper idea. Now the whole store gets involved because of what Josh and MacMillan exude."

Stroman worked with her assistants on dance steps and props in September's pre-production sessions and, yesterday, they tried it again with actors Jenkins and Cypher. The group ran through many of the steps the full cast will do today, playing piano keys with their hands, feet, butts and entire bodies. Jenkins tried a handstand at one point, a glissando across the keys on a pink skateboard at another.

Today, production assistants push the keyboard into the center of the rehearsal room. Starting with Jenkins and Cypher, Stroman adds lines of dancers standing and jumping onto the keyboard. They sit on the keys, lie across them, drag a leg, drag one another.

At the piano, Krane says, "Let's try it a little faster," and they do. Perfectly. Is that as fast as it gets? "Almost," he smiles.

The dancers are seated at one point, rump-to-rump, kids and adults, at the top of the keyboard. Stroman faces them, hands on her waist, eyes lost in space. It is her most frequent pose. The choreographer experiments: "Enrico, why don't you try hitting with your hand on the second key? Joyce, try hitting the first key with your left heel."

When rehearsal ends, actor Ray Wills says in a stage whisper, "That's the number that will stop the Tonys." More correctly, as time will tell, that's the number they'll be very lucky to get *on* the Tonys.

Monday, December 18, 1995

Big trucks start unloading at the Fisher Theatre in De-

troit.

Tuesday, December 19, 1995

Bachelor party for Ockrent at an Italian restaurant on West 46th St. Maybe 20 guys, including Tim Rice and Alan Menken as well as a *Big* contingent, are on hand for a selection of songs with dirty and/or clever lyrics. Among the names Maltby and Shire found to rhyme with Stroman: Willy Loman and Jane Froman. The Ockrent rhyme is less exotic, less lyrical and a great deal cruder.

Tuesday, December 26, 1995

Problems continue with the end of the first act. It still has the wrong feel, Ockrent says, and everybody has gone back to the drawing board. "There's always one section of a show that's hard to crack," Stroman says, "and it will probably take the whole rehearsal process to crack it."

Saturday, December 30, 1995

Ockrent and Stroman are in "wedding panic" prior to tomorrow's nuptials. Ockrent says he plans to "get past it and on with the show. Then back to honeymooning."

Sunday, December 31, 1995

Stroman and Ockrent get married at the Stanhope Hotel. The evening sweeps in dinner, dancing and fireworks. "It looked like the opening night of a Broadway show," Wagner reports. "A lot of celebrities dressed up in penguin suits."

1996

Thursday, January 4, 1996

Jenkins has acute laryngitis and, with group sales presentations next week, is told to rest his voice. So understudy Vlastnik reads Jenkins' lines while Jenkins mimes them. "It's like working with Marcel Marceau," says Ockrent.

If nothing else, it takes attention off the gnawing problem of how to end the first act. MacMillan's annual office party has long been established as the setting for the last scene,

but what exactly happens at that party has been in constant flux. Lines change. Songs change. Dances change.

Their goal is to conclude the act with some metaphor for Josh's choice between adulthood and childhood, and the newest solution involves his teen crush, Cynthia Benson. Ockrent has now concluded that when Josh kisses Susan, what immediately comes into his mind is the luminous Benson. So they've put that thought onstage, choreographing a dance solo for Benson.

Even as they set the act's new ending in place, however, everyone knows it's temporary. There's no haunting duet, no big production number, nothing to send the audience out to intermission enchanted. Instead there is a solitary ballerina dancing around a leading man who wears a flashy white suit, yet is strangely silent and immobile.

Friday, January 5, 1996

New York Times "On Stage, and Off" previews spring Broadway offerings. Noting all the revivals, columnist Peter Marks calls *Big* the "Great White Way Hope." Ockrent is quoted saying, "What I hope is there is a resurgence of new musicals. If shows like this succeed, it can only encourage it."

Saturday, January 6, 1996, London

Mike Ockrent's son, Ben, now 14, has been advising his father on teenagers. Ben and a friend made a tape of music that teenagers listen to, including selections of Pearl Jam, Snoop Doggy Dog, Ice-T and Body Count. Ben, who lives here with his mother, Susan Ockrent, answers all his father's questions by phone, fax and e-mail.

When he was 13 and "it was easy for me to see things through Josh's point of view," the show's Special Consultant to the Director on Adolescent Affairs put together a list of things a 13-year-old could not do. Among them: go out to nightclubs, drive, live on your own, be taken seriously, go to adult-rated movies.

Ben is actually a little embarrassed about that list today, thinking it naive. Then again, he is a pretty sophisticated kid. Ockrent senior jokes that his tombstone will read, "He had

more air miles than sense," and Ben has done his share of travelling as well. He has acted professionally, including a run as Gavroche in *Les Misérables* on the West End, and looks a lot more like Hugh Grant than Mike Ockrent.

But Ben does express a typical teen's pride in impressing and assisting so significant an adult in his life. "I like the experience of helping him," Ben says, "although while I'm around him, I know that whatever I do, I'm being noted. So I have to think of my fellow adolescents before I do something."

What might he, a prototypical adolescent, have in his pockets, Ben is asked. His father says 13- and 14-year-olds have great things in their pockets. Emptying first his pants pockets, then his jacket pockets onto a table, Ben makes a heap of coins, candy wrappers, Kleenex, basketball game timetables and a ticket stub for the film *French Kiss*.

Then he smiles. "My father didn't tell me about that theory."

Sunday, January 7, 1996

Crazy for You closes today at the Shubert Theatre after 1,643 performances. Its longevity reinforces the magic of playing the Shubert Theatre: *A Chorus Line* closed there April 28, 1990, after nearly 15 years and 6,137 performances.

Monday, January 8, 1996

Major blizzard, but nearly everyone shows up for rehearsal. Says Ockrent: "Washington closed down, but *Big* went on."

Many of its suppliers did not, however, which will later tighten an already tight schedule.

Tuesday, January 9, 1996

Group sales presentations today and Thursday showcase excerpts from the show. Invitations promise, "Some big songs, big laughs and big fun." It's a chance to "be among the first to see the musical sure to make everyone feel 10 feet tall."

These mini-productions get the word out to the people who organize group theater parties around the New York area.

"Hopefully they start pre-booking," says Ockrent. "They can add a million dollars to your box office in one fell swoop."

Wednesday, January 10, 1996

Designer David Peterson at Robin Wagner's studio considers this to be the most nerve-wracking time. The last scenery and props trucks will head out in a few weeks, and Peterson worries every time a call comes in from Detroit.

Can they make changes after this? "We can do anything with time and money," Peterson replies. "But if there isn't enough time, we need more money."

Monday, January 15, 1996

Variety has front-page story headlined "B'way braces for 'Big' one." Second paragraph notes the show "will represent the most ambitious merchandising blitz ever to hit the Street." Besides selling theater tickets at its Fifth Avenue flagship, F.A.O. Schwarz will sell 62 *Big*-related products at the Shubert Theatre and in its many stores.

Never mind that in this campaign *Big* is following the well-trod path of *Batman* movies, Lloyd Webber musicals and even the Public Broadcasting Service's *Sesame Street*. *Big* is taken to task from the start. *Variety* reporter Jeremy Gerard raises what he calls "a key question" and one that will color the show's press coverage from this day on: "All of this is good for business, but what about art?"

Freydberg says he understands what is happening. "Somehow or other, the theater press thinks that theater, even commercial theater, should not be commercial. I think they view it as an art form and get incensed when they see it commercialized. But this is a natural tie-in."

Tuesday, January 16, 1996

Open rehearsal for the press. Eight pizzas, large, are consumed. More than 30 reporters, cameramen and others line the rehearsal room for a sampler of ballads and production numbers. "Fun," the piano keyboard number, will get considerable airplay over the next few days, and television coverage

nearly always includes footage from the film as well. One television reporter asks Crista Moore whether or not the show can live up to its name. She replies that she thinks so.

Wednesday, January 17, 1996

Weidman sends fax to Ockrent taking out many dirty words. No more "Shit!" when little Josh slams down his skateboard; now it's "Leave me alone!" Executive Paul no longer calls big Josh "a back-stabbing little shit." Now he's a "backstabbing little snake." A "little scumbag" becomes a "little weasel." Weidman explains later that when he was listening to the show the other day, he was staggered by how many foul words there were. It was all he heard. So he decided to take some of them out. He calls the fax "Expletives Deleted."

Thursday, January 18, 1996

Cocktail party tonight at F.A.O. Schwarz before everyone heads off for Detroit.

FAO's display model of the piano keyboard has been set up downstairs should anyone care to dance on it, and Eyler can't resist. Cypher arrives early and catches Eyler dancing on the keys all by himself "and smiling with enormous pleasure."

Eyler later takes Cypher and other actors to his office. He shows them a mock-up of the new *Big* keyboard toy that will sport six of the show's songs embedded on a chip. Shire says it's a milestone for a composer to see his work on a chip.

Eyler thinks the new toy, a steal at $42, will sell well. He also expects the store to move a lot of *Big* boxer shorts.

Tuesday, January 23, 1996

Patrick Levis' 14th birthday. His parents, whom he hasn't seen since New Year's, surprise him by coming up from Maryland for his birthday party. The WOR-TV camera crew captures it all on film.

What the cameramen will miss is his coming growth spurt, which will require moving the huge carnival hand upward three

times so Josh is still too small for the Wild Thunder ride. (No rejection at Wild Thunder, no need for a wish, no story.) Levis, who says he hopes the show runs long enough for him to play big Josh, will soon have to stoop to be shorter than the other kids.

Wednesday, January 24, 1996

New song today. Maltby and Shire finished it at 12:30 this morning, Stroman says. They came over, Ockrent fed them Chinese food and wouldn't let them out of the house until they were done. He actually went off to bed before they finished, she adds.

10:00 am

Cast gathers to sing "The New Guy," a song that characterizes how MacMillan Toys executives react to the boss' new favorite, Josh.

Stroman walks them through the number, showing them how to turn to the audience, each other and, finally, as they sing the refrain, to Josh. As they rehearse, Maltby revises his lyrics. At one point, the actors are at the piano singing one lyric for the song and Maltby is standing right next to them singing a whole new lyric.

2:40 pm

Afternoon run-through. As he sets up the opening scenes, Ockrent mutters, "Baby rattles. Roller coasters. Magic castles. I used to direct Strindberg."

6:00 pm

Rehearsal ends.

"So often, work is horizontal," says Weidman. "You do things over and make them different. Not better but different. The past 10 days, we've been pushing it in the right direction. It doesn't make you feel any less tired, but it does make you feel as though it was worth it."

Ockrent says it's "like the curate's egg. When somebody asked the curate how his egg was, he said, 'Good. In parts.'"

The director pauses, gives a wan smile. "You have to be English."

9:45 pm

Weidman and Ockrent meet at Ockrent's place. Ockrent cooks, then eats pasta and chicken as Weidman reads aloud his notes from today's run-through. He has many concerns, but Ockrent prefers to wait on some decisions until Detroit to see audience reaction.

Weidman: "Do you want a laugh there?"

Ockrent: "When we have too many laughs, we'll cut it."

10:00 pm

Tonight's plan is to sharpen an exchange between Paul, the nasty toy company executive, and his boss, MacMillan. Paul currently offers up a new toy—"baby's first bar set"— that plays off the little bottles served on airplanes and that always gets a laugh. Lines have been "Try a martini, spelled t-e-e-n-y" and "How 'bout mar-<u>tiny</u>," but the two men want to improve on the joke. How can they extend it without killing it?

10:45 pm

Ockrent goes to his liquor cabinet, opens it and desperately looks at the bottles for inspiration.

11:45 pm

Weidman finally goes home. They have a solution.

Thursday, January 25, 1996

Media deluge. Susan Stamberg is doing interviews for National Public Radio's *All Things Considered* in one rehearsal room, a television camera crew has set up shop in a second, and a reporter from *Newsday* is shadowing one of the local kids for a newspaper feature. Boneau/Bryan-Brown sends a fax almost every day requesting an interview or photo, and this week the publicity firm is delivering giant white cups with red *Big* lettering to some 300 press people. Press activity will only accelerate as the Broadway opening gets closer.

10:00 am

Maltby and Shire visit a third record company talking possible deals for the *Big* cast album. Each company has gone all-out, bringing in major players, sweetening offers. Phil Ramone, "the Pope of Pop," is at rehearsals today to talk to Maltby and Shire, and they hope he will want to produce the album. (He does.)

1:00 pm

Lunch break in the rapidly-filling costume area. Empty shopping bags from Macy's, Brooks Bros., Saks, the Limited, Banana Republic and elsewhere are against the wall, and costumers continue their work as the creative team has its usual lunch-hour meeting. Ockrent and Weidman rehash the "baby's first bar-set" sequence.

4:00 pm

Weidman is back. MacMillan will say, "Are you suggesting we sell liquor to children?" and Paul will respond: "Nobody else is doing it." Weidman hands the new page over to Ockrent who takes a look, nods his head and has Cypher and Gene Weygandt, who plays Paul, read it aloud. "Done deal," Ockrent decides. "We're moving on."

4:45 pm

Moore feels she's just about mastered Susan's intricate new song, "I'll Think About It Later." "It's pattery," she says, "and there are so many similar words, and it's so fast, it's tough to memorize. I was in the tub last night with this, going over and over it. I don't know if it was because it was so late, but I was having a really hard time."

5:00 pm

Ockrent has a new script page for Moore. Only a lyric change, he smiles. Moore rushes out of the room.

Friday, January 26

Meeting at Serino Coyne to discuss advertising strategy.

Advance sales so far haven't been impressive, despite a big *New York Times* ad last Sunday and a recent promotional offer through Bloomingdale's. Next up is a direct mail campaign, mostly to theater subscribers, and Freydberg says he expects more action in February.

Producers, publicists and advertising people discuss national advertising. Agency executives expect that in six months, 40% of *Big*'s audience will be from out of town. In 12 months, that will climb to 60%.

They recommend commercial–maker Steve Horn to Freydberg and play Horn's television ads for *Cats*, *Grand Hotel* and other clients. He also did the television ad for Feld's Ringling Bros. Agency advice: Horn's expensive but worth it.

"There are two kinds of commercials," says Feld, a soft-spoken, well-tailored man who looks more like a banker than a circus king. "One is artistic and wonderful but may not get your message across. The other is not. Horn's commercial featuring the circus didn't succeed in selling tickets. It reinforced what people already knew. I signed off on it—it was beautiful. But we had to redo it and cut it differently.

"It's a blessing and a curse that people know *Big*. If you go out and survey people, they know the piano scene. So that's the expectation. Yes, you have to allude to it. You satisfy that. Then you show them things they didn't expect—the relationship, the romance."

Saturday, January 27, 1996

Last run-through today before Detroit. Maybe 100 people are on hand, most of them theater professionals. Tabisel says he expects his mother to cry through the whole show. (She does.)

Response is good. Freddie Gershon, chairman and owner of the licensing agency Music Theatre International, says, "The last time a musical got me to cry like this was *A Chorus Line*. Someone has a vision here." Summarizes Shire: "I heard laughter. I heard applause. I saw a few handkerchiefs."

Ockrent is more cautious in his analysis. "The scary thing is to not let the sets, costumes and props swamp all this energy," he says. "What I saw today had all the energy and pace.

It's also a very friendly house. You never know until you get to Detroit in front of an audience that's spent $70."

To end the day, the director gives both notes and praise to his cast. "The show is really coming together now, and has exactly the right feel," he tells them. "This is the end of the first stage, and you are an incredible company to have come through all of this. A new musical is one of the hardest things you do in the theater, and our doing it is a tribute to all of us."

Everyone gives everyone else a standing ovation. Then, keeping with tradition on Zweigbaum's shows, the cast pulls up all the colored tape on the rehearsal room floor and makes it into a ball for Zweigbaum's desk in Detroit.

Monday, January 29, 1996

Two Olympia Trails buses—one with a huge banner saying, "Leaving for *Big* Fun in Detroit—Back to Broadway on April 2!"—are parked alongside the Shubert Theatre in Shubert Alley at 9:00 a.m., waiting to take cast and crew to Newark Airport.

Well-wishers are gathered for the send-off. Among them is Mel Gross, Greenblatt's college roommate and an investor in the show. Streit's matzo is his family business, and for him, his mother and sister, *Big* marks their first venture into theatrical investment. Greenblatt was best man at Gross' first wedding, and, says Gross, "I hope this runs longer than that did." How long would that be? Twelve years.

The press contingent includes NY1, a 24-hour all-news channel. "We are anticipating that *Big* will be the big musical of the year," says entertainment reporter Sharon Dizenhuz. "Because of its success as a movie, it will generate a lot of attention—just being at the Shubert Theatre creates an impression of having a lock on success."

Freydberg is more restrained, at least publicly. "Now we're heading for the judgment day," he says. "It's wonderful, this dream of all convincing ourselves that we have something. But what if the people out there who buy the tickets don't agree? What if we're deluding ourselves? It's the moment of truth—if what we're seeing is what they're seeing."

PART THREE:
DETROIT

"If you put Richard and me in a room with a piano and three monkeys with a typewriter for the age of the universe, it's just possible that we might come up with the right first number for Susan Lawrence before the monkeys type Hamlet."

—David Shire, composer,

March 6, 1996

DETROIT

THEY don't call it Murder City anymore, but Detroit sure isn't Fun City either. This is a depressed industrial town in the dead of winter.

Big general manager Robert Kamlot compares sending a show out of town to setting up bivouac, with people, trucks and show innards trekking inland for weeks. "There are no diversions, no family or friends to go home to," he adds. "You're just there to work."

Most of the cast and crew stay at the St. Regis Hotel, built in French chateau-style and located about three miles from downtown Detroit. The hotel is connected by skywalks to a mall and then to three office buildings. One of them is the Fisher Building, a beautiful art deco structure designed by Albert Kahn, built in 1928 and home to the 2,089-seat Fisher Theatre.

The Fisher was a movie palace until 1961, and its chandeliers and ornate mezzanine curtains speak of palmier times. Gone are the live birds in cages and live fish in pools downstairs, leaving behind vast expanses of lower lobby filled with just a few pieces of furniture and a candy seller at showtime.

Given the neighborhood—known locally by some as the DMZ—and the winter weather, most of the company has little, if any, exposure to natural light or air during this period. Aside from stops at the hotel gym, where cast member CJay Hardy sometimes teaches aerobics classes to colleagues, the only offstage exercise is the eight-minute walk from the hotel through the mall to the theater each day.

Inside the auditorium, it is nearly always night, as lighting is among the last elements to be added. The huge lighting team is always there, from early morning to late at night, but even after rehearsals start, most of the show's action still appears to be occurring sometime in the middle of the night.

In all that darkness, Ockrent seems like the unseen director in *A Chorus Line* as he calls out to his cast, his voice amplified through a microphone on his work table. Except,

of course, he's rarely at that work table; more often, he's rushing onstage to move an actor, adjust a scene or deal with some terrible set crisis.

Joseph Nederlander has essentially turned his office over to Ockrent. It is in the lower lobby, just down the hall from the men's room, and has no windows. Maltby and Shire work primarily in Shire's hotel suite, but Weidman, who is staying at a hotel some distance away, has set up camp in the windowless, airless room. As problems mount, people start referring to it as "the bunker."

Big is a show about time, and time is the show's most implacable opponent. The set is so complicated, the schedule so delayed by the January blizzards, that Ockrent doesn't really see his show until its audiences do. "He never had a complete run-through before the first performance," says producer Mark. "In a way, we discovered the show was in trouble along with the audiences."

Jon Cypher recalls that even Rodgers and Hammerstein didn't relish out-of-town, pre-Broadway tryouts with shows they knew had problems. "The audience will tell you about new problems, and you'll never have the chance to fix the problems you had," says Cypher. "All you have is five hours a day to rehearse. You can't work matinees, and you have Mondays off. So you really have 20 hours a week to fix whatever you think's wrong, and that ain't much."

Thursday, February 1, 1996, Detroit

Cast moves into Fisher Theatre after two days of rehearsal at the Masonic Temple Theatre a few miles away. The Fisher launched such hit shows as *Hello, Dolly!, Fiddler on the Roof* and *The Wiz*, and Stroman tells a local reporter that "it means Detroit has good theater karma."

Soon the theater's auditorium looks like theater auditoriums usually look during rehearsals. Tables cover chunks of seats, then are laden with laptop computers, monitors, notebooks, junk food and assorted personal effects of the set, lighting, costume and other production people who work at the tables day after day. Before the show goes into previews, the

tables are there around the clock, but once performances start, they must be disassembled each afternoon, then reassembled each morning.

There are dancers in the lobby and lower lobby, pianos on the mezzanine, and props stacked up by the subscription sales office. Understudies rehearse near the stairwell, and music copyists do their meticulous, hand-written copying at tables set up in a storage room downstairs. The theater's large second elevator, now stationary, has been turned into a production office, where company manager Steven Chaikelson keeps a plant for needed oxygen; he is often barely visible behind all the winter coats and briefcases tossed into the tiny room during performances.

Nederlander has high hopes for the Fisher's new tenant. "This show is demographically perfect," he says. "People are sick and tired of smut and dirt."

Friday, February 2, 1996, Detroit

New York Times announces that the Joseph Papp Public Theater/New York Shakespeare Festival will take its hit show, *Bring in 'da Noise, Bring in 'da Funk*, to Broadway. The tap/rap musical, created by Savion Glover and George C. Wolfe, was a sell-out during its three month run downtown. It will open April 25.

Spring line-up has begun to change.

Saturday, February 3, 1996, Detroit

Ockrent decides to cut "Say Good Morning to Mom," a jazzy song that Mrs. Baskin sings in her kitchen while Josh is still sleeping, neither of them yet aware of his metamorphosis. Maltby and Shire wrote the song to establish the ordinariness of the day, or as Maltby puts it, they took the notion of Mrs. Baskin humming and expanded it into a song.

"Mother is humming downstairs, he wakes up, and this extraordinary thing is happening," says Maltby. "It seems so unlikely he'd be so articulate as to look in the mirror and immediately express his reactions in words. It's an oblique way of dealing with the [situation]."

There is no time for obliqueness so early in the show, however. Ockrent wants to move quickly to Josh's discovery that he's a big guy now. The song has to go.

Barbara Walsh still gets to sing the well-received song, "Stop, Time," but the actress readily admits frustration that a role small to begin with has become smaller. "We had worked on the new scene without the song, and I pretended it didn't bother me," Walsh says later. "But when we were discussing it with the creators, I just started crying. I told Mike very honestly what I felt—that 'Stop, Time's' impact is lessened or dissipated by not having that song. It provides information and sets up the relationship between Josh and his mother. It means the song is earned."

"Say Good Morning to Mom" also acted as a bridge into the show's title tune—a song in which Josh reacts to his new stature not with delight at being a grown-up, but rather with horror. Its departure moved up the song, "Big," and, as everyone was to learn, caused a whole new set of problems. After the change was made, Maltby remembers, "John Weidman asked me if it was a smart idea or a catastrophe, and I felt it was both."

Monday, February 5, 1996, Detroit

Ockrent scraps the school bathroom scene where adult Josh first reveals his new identity to pal Billy. The bathroom set cost upwards of $5,000 "but it was way underdesigned," Wagner says later. "I always thought we would lose that scene, so I didn't spend a lot of time and money on it. All Billy had to do was come out of the house. It doesn't have to be so site specific."

Wednesday, February 7, 1996, Detroit

Jon Cypher sings national anthem at the Detroit Pistons/ Orlando Magic basketball game. It may have been 25 years since he last sang on Broadway, but it's only been a few months since he last sang the anthem in Pittsburgh, Pennsylvania.

In Hershey, Pennsylvania, meanwhile, producer Jonathan Herzog of *State Fair* goes onstage to tell the audience that the show is headed for Broadway. It will begin performances

March 20 (and be bolstered later by a $1 million investment from legendary producer David Merrick).

Thursday, February 8, 1996, Detroit

Dinner tonight, as most nights, is at Il Centro, a nearby Italian bistro where paper tablecloths and crayons are often used to make notes about the show or work out frustrations in strange and wondrous drawings. Maltby is reading aloud from the potential program, calling out song names and set locations. Decisions include whether to call Tavern on the Green a "New York restaurant" or "Tavern on the Green." (They go with "New York restaurant" to keep the set a surprise for the audience.)

Rehearsals continue after dinner. Ockrent says, "We're not out of the woods yet," but visiting producer Greenblatt sees only success: "Every time I think this show is as good as it can be, it gets better. This will definitely be my last show—nothing can top this. I'll go and produce movies."

Friday, February 9, 1996, Detroit

Out in the Fisher Theatre lobby, somebody is restuffing the life-size toy reindeer; it is too soft. The bears will be next.

1:00 pm

Time for the *sitzprobe,* when orchestra and cast first perform the score together. Nicholas Archer, the show's associate conductor, compares the moment to going from black-and-white television to color.

The orchestra has assembled in the theater lobby, and many cast members take photographs of the musicians before settling themselves nearby on the stairs. It is an intimate setting and an emotional one; several actors are on the verge of tears as they sing their songs for the first time to full accompaniment. "We've been doing it in a rehearsal room with a piano," Crista Moore says. "Now the reality hits you."

6:00 pm

Dinner hour. The writers are talking about their lives at home, their sense of being away and out of the loop. Maltby

recites Maltby's Rule: "If you are lucky enough to be involved in a musical, the price you pay is that your private life will completely fall apart. If there's illness possible, it will happen. Twice I went into rehearsal, and my father had a heart attack the first day of each."

Ockrent says he thought of his own children today when he heard Barbara Walsh sing "Stop, Time," a ballad about the stages of a child's life, and it seems nearly everyone at the table did. Maltby, whose five children range in age from 2 to 28, is particularly attached to the song and its theme that "you're constantly saying goodbye to children you've fallen in love with."

Walsh sings: "Birthdays fly/ Seven, eight, nine, ten/ Ev'ry kid he becomes/ You clutch and say 'Stop, Time'/ Hold this one fast/ But it's not supposed to last/ And that time has come and passed/ For he's growing and he has to go."

These are family men, people whose wives and children visit rehearsals and performances in Detroit as well as in New York, and, in the case of Ockrent and Shire, whose sons are even credited in the show's program as consultants. It is one reason why this material has such a strong hold on them.

Saturday, February 10, 1996, Detroit

Stroman dreams that Ockrent says none of the dances are working, and he's going to bring in the Rockettes.

1:00 pm

Ockrent comes to rehearsal carrying large shopping bags. There's a one-day sale at Crowley's, the department store in the mall, and he discovered it was cheaper to buy new socks and underwear than to pay for laundry at the hotel. Several cast members rush over as well, including Cypher, who causes a stir when shoppers spot a major television star.

Big's star today is costume designer William Ivey Long. He is a nicely-dressed Southern gentleman who introduced himself the first day of rehearsal as "a Virgo—organized and insane" and later confides, "I'm an SOB—I state the obvious."

Since the set is more or less in place, costumes are next. "That's how you work, by necessity," explains the de-

signer. "On *Guys and Dolls*, for instance, Tony Walton created Runyonland, then I populated it and Paul Gallo illuminated it. You have to know the architecture and what the surrounding landscape looks like. The Garden of Eden was there first—then came Adam and Eve and the snake."

Example: Moore's trench coat in the show's final warehouse scene. "It's the *Casablanca* moment," Long says. "They're in an airplane hanger, and she's saying goodbye. She's not going off with him, and they're sacrificing personal happiness for each other."

As for all the people who inhabit Wagner's New Jersey neighborhood, Long says that to avoid playing into New Jersey jokes, he's really doing Connecticut. And remember, he adds, "it's all seen through the eyes of a 13-year-old. Children don't see nuance, so I have to help the audience with a larger-than-life vision."

Aside from dressing Zoltar, the mysterious carnival figure that grants Josh's wish to be big, Long has a limited, contemporary palette on this show. Yet he still needs clothes that will read in the back of the house (where associate costume designer Scott Traugott often sits with binoculars to check up on shoes, hose and accessories). Once he's a corporate star, Josh wears Armani-like suits, and many of his executive colleagues are also swathed in designer look-alikes. Kids' clothes are usually bought ready-made, and Traugott is often out shopping Detroit and Ann Arbor malls for costumes.

Assembling *Big*'s wardrobe took substantial planning. Each cast member has been given a number, and those numbers, actors' names and the act and scene in which each costume appears have been put on a label and sewn in every garment. Whenever possible, the clothes are in the appropriate dressing room, set up in order of appearance.

All that will help the crew of dressers who appear for the first time tonight. Most of the dressers are local, although a few have come in from New York, and haven't met either the cast or their costumes. Getting to know them all will take some time, both here and back in New York.

Consider John Sloman, a member of the ensemble who has so many costume changes that dresser Ocean Gray rarely

leaves his side offstage. Sloman is "underdressed"—a theatrical term for clothes layering—during much of the first act. When he appears as a bum in the Port Authority scene, his overcoat hides his costumes for the next several scenes. He wears five pairs of socks at once to accompany all those changes.

9:00 pm

Costume rehearsal starts. Opening scenes, which had seemed fine back in the rehearsal hall, now seem slow and endless. But script problems take a back seat to technical problems right now. One of the New Jersey houses doesn't turn properly, and other set pieces move across the stage like they're plowing through Jell-O.

The actors, however, can't move fast enough. There isn't much room backstage, the cast is huge and the costume changes continual. As new scenes start, some actors make it onstage in time but others don't. Both script and score will wind up being adjusted to accommodate costume changes.

What's it like backstage now? Think Vietnam, suggests Ray Wills, who plays a clown, a businessman, a yuppie and a bum. "It's like the fall of Saigon back there. You don't know which are the Viet Cong or if you'll get hit by friendly fire."

Things take time, explains stage manager Zweigbaum at the end of a three-hour first act. "It's like any other major construction; it doesn't just happen. Every part has to be worked on. The crew's learning. Then we introduce dressers, and there's no room for them. But because we know it will work, we're not pulling our hair out."

Not yet.

Sunday, February 11, 1996, Detroit

Two days until first preview, and this time Long has the nightmare. He dreams that he left his apartment with the shower running. "It woke me right up," he says.

Wigs are going in along with the costumes today, and they, too, are more difficult on a contemporary show. "There are no guidelines," explains Ray Marston, the London-based

wigmaker who also worked on *Sunset Boulevard* and *Les Misérables*. "On a period show, you can just look at a history book, and it's all there."

The process on *Big* is more complicated. Long briefs the hair and wig staff on how he wants everyone to look—tart, brassy, upper-class, etc. The collaborators choose hair color and styles, then prepare a sheet for each character, attaching a photograph of a suggested hairstyle. (Donna Lee Marshall's "shopper" photo, for instance, is of a smiling Hillary Rodham Clinton.) The character summaries and photos are sent along to Marston's, where wigs are handcrafted of human hair.

What looks great on a mannequin in Marston's Covent Garden studio can look dreary onstage, however. "Light changes everything," says David Brian Brown, the show's hair and wig designer. "Highlights might be too subtle or too bright."

But that, on a larger scale, is why they're in Detroit. "We'll be thrilled if we go back to New York having addressed all of the major and most of the minor problems," Weidman says. "For three and a half years, we've been our own audience. This is the Rubicon. Suddenly you're going to have [thousands of] people to give you information."

Tonight they receive other information as well—new investors. Kyodo Tokyo, a diversified entertainment firm, had executive producer Yoshito Yamazaki hanging around rehearsals all weekend, and he liked what he saw. This evening he phoned the president of his company back in Japan and got a go-ahead to invest in the show. Contract signings at 11:00 here tonight will be followed by more in New York in the morning. A Japanese production in association with Fuji Television is anticipated for Tokyo in 1998.

Monday, February 12, 1996, Detroit

One day until what Ockrent calls "our first performance for paying guests."

Cast and crew are still becoming familiar with how, where and when set pieces are stacked above the stage and lowered by computer cues as needed. Maltby comments that what took 45 minutes to do onstage in *Miss Saigon* the first week, took 15 minutes the second.

2:00 pm

Run-through starts.

2:07 pm

Run-through stops when a side panel comes down early.

2:30 pm

Overkill on dry ice for magic effect. So much stage smoke is pouring into the orchestra pit that Gemignani can't see his score, and the musicians can't see him.

3:45 pm

Actors can't get out of the onstage houses to exit the scene. Somebody forgot to unlock the doors.

5:45 pm

Backstage crew reports in, using words like "chaos" and "mayhem."

11:10 pm

End of rehearsal. Ockrent tells the cast he just may cancel the first preview.

What he doesn't tell them yet is that he and Freydberg have decided to let the press in one night early. They hear critics are griping about losing a big chunk of the three-day holiday weekend if there's a Friday press opening. Says Freydberg, "You don't want the press coming in annoyed. And what's the difference between Thursday and Friday? We're not ready anyway."

Tuesday, February 13, 1996, Detroit

First preview tonight.

The blackout drop that goes behind the front curtain hasn't arrived, and the temporary replacement is a clingy fabric in an auditorium known for drafts. The set is so complicated and mishaps still so frequent that nearly everyone expects things to grind to a halt at some unpredictable moment during the performance.

Meanwhile, back in New York, two events are occuring that will soon affect them. In the short term, another blizzard has shut down airports and will keep family, friends and backers from attending this first performance. But what is of far more importance to their collective futures is the Off Broadway opening, at the 150-seat New York Theatre Workshop in the East Village, of Jonathan Larson's new rock opera, *Rent*.

1:50 pm

Run-through starts. Less than five minutes into the show, one of the onstage houses doesn't turn. Ockrent is out of his seat, incredulous; it is the same computer screwup as three days before. It is only a two-minute delay, but another soon occurs. Backstage people say they need more time, more technical rehearsals.

Wills comes to the front of the stage. He and other cast members are having trouble getting Vlastnik, the guy in the giant bear costume, offstage fast enough; it's so dark between scenes that they can't find his head, let alone an armpit. Ockrent suggests they close their eyes and try it a few times that way to get the feel of doing it in the dark.

4:30 pm

Sets collide. The elevator that moves the huge F.A.O. Schwarz clock tower down under the stage was not flush with the floor when it stopped, so a unit coming onstage bumped into it. "Two objects cannot occupy the same space at the same time," observes Wagner. "We've never quite made peace with that in the theater."

6:00 pm

Orchestration arrives for the curtain call. "Standard," Maltby says, unconcerned. "Usually it comes in at 7. We're an hour early."

The secret to surviving opening night, says Wagner, "is to look for order in the chaos. Without chaos, it's not exciting."

8:05 pm

Show time. Ockrent comes onstage to welcome the audi-

ence to the show's very first performance. His microphone doesn't work.

"Welcome to a little bit of theater history," he eventually tells them. "We hope it won't go wrong, but it may."

8:12 pm

One of the houses onstage spins but doesn't move forward. The curtain comes down, and a voice booms out: "Ladies and gentlemen, we're experiencing technical difficulties. We'll be right back."

A man rises from his seat and heads up the aisle and out. Weidman is mournful: "Once people get up and start moving around, you might as well give up."

8:30 pm

Show resumes. (A cable-bearing wheel pulled loose, and stagehands had to remove part of the stage floor, fix the problem, then put the stage floor back.)

11:20 pm

Show ends to polite applause, and a few people even spring to their feet in appreciation. The evening is a benefit for Independence for Life, a program that provides low-cost transportation to groups serving Michigan's elderly, and such groups are traditionally more difficult to please. Concludes Freydberg: "Pretty damn good for a benefit audience."

12:00 midnight

Ockrent and the creative team return to the St. Regis, are applauded by cast members partying in the bar and move on to set up camp in the overly-lit lobby.

The director flips open his notebook and reads: Motivation isn't clear. Title song isn't great. Need more back-story on MacMillan. Loft scene is a mess. Yuppie scene isn't much better.

Among Ockrent's suggestions is something "quieter" for the title song; not only is it Josh's first song as a grown-up, but it introduces Jenkins "and is full of dramatic content."

An offstage chorus isn't working right, timing is off on the lead-in to the Port Authority scene, and Jenkins seems frantic as he tries to exit that scene and open the next at F.A.O. Schwarz. They need to figure out a better way to get all the chunks of the giant keyboard onstage once the dance number starts.

Also worrisome is MacMillan's story. His problems with MacMillan Toys are currently "our little secret," Maltby jokes. To be decided: should the information come in a line or a lyric? And what can they do to make the Magic Castle "more of a Preston Sturges moment" as it was in the rehearsal room?

1:45 am

Cast party is still going strong in the bar. Creative team is still dishing the show in the lobby. Ockrent finishes with his notepad and moves on to note cards. Everybody else has red, watery eyes.

2:00 am

Coffee table is covered with crumpled note cards. Meeting is adjourned.

Wednesday, February 14, 1996, Detroit

First major controversy.

Ockrent gets a call at 9:00 a.m. that producer Feld is upset about the scene where young and old Josh share the stage. Young Josh is imagining his first sexual experience in the song "I Want to Know," while the adult Josh and Susan are getting more and more intimate a few feet away. Currently, the adult Josh tentatively touches Susan's breast—a gesture that was also in the film—and Feld has conveyed, via Freydberg, that the scene could wreak havoc upon his primary business of providing family entertainment.

A few hours later, when Ockrent meets with his creative team to discuss book problems, talk keeps going back to what all of them consider possible "censorship." The way Ockrent explains it, a request has come from Feld, via Freydberg, to cut the hand-on-the-breast moment.

Never mind that Patrick Buchanan won the Iowa primary yesterday. This comes from nowhere, and they seem quite stunned. Feld apparently didn't complain about Josh rushing for a pillow to cover an erection the first time he falls on Susan, about the kids calling each other "asshole," about the basic premise of romance between a 13-year-old boy and a 30ish woman.

The issue had been building, it turns out. There had been complaints about the scene after the group sales presentation. Then, at the first preview, Feld heard a woman say she liked the show but wouldn't send her friends because of the breast touching.

They go around the issue, alternating comic relief—put her in a parka—with great solemnity. Maltby, who also got a call from Freydberg that morning, is somewhat willing to compromise. Is there a way of showing that tenderness without being so "startling?" he asks.

But neither Maltby nor anyone else suggests cutting the moment itself. "It would be anaesthetizing and sanitizing the show to the point that we'd be laughed at," Ockrent says. "In the movie, it is *the* moment—the essence of the 13-year-old—which is what this show is about. She turns off the light, and he turns it on."

Weidman had already, on his own, eliminated many a foul word. (See "Expletives Deleted" fax of January 17.) Now they hear that Feld also objects to the word "balls" in the lyric: "I love this guy. Does he have balls or what?" which is sung about Josh by MacMillan. (It will be changed to "guts," and, later, "brass," and, later still, back to "balls" again.)

1:30 pm

Rehearsal starts. Ockrent tells Jenkins and Moore to change the seduction scene a little. She shouldn't unbutton her sweater. She should take his hand and put it outside her shirt. Jenkins: "Too much sex education for the kids, huh?"

As Freydberg explains later, he, Mark and the rest of the producing team viewed the project as family entertainment.

90

"At the first group presentation, lots of people were really upset about the fact that Dan touched Crista's breast. Now, this week, some very vocal audience members, maybe eight of them, ask to see the producers. [F.A.O. Schwarz executive] Eyler also felt it was not in good taste, and it is the first time he has ever made an artistic comment on the show. Although it was done onscreen, it is different when it is live. I thought it was a dramatic, wonderful scene, but I also clearly understand their strong feelings."

6:20 pm

Talk of the controversial scene continues over dinner. Ockrent says everyone has to back him up on a decision, and Shire, Maltby and Weidman all agree to do so. The director is very passionate, his face flushed: "It is the *heart* of the show. It's the only moment we've got, and this is what I told Ken Feld."

11:00 pm

After tonight's second preview, there's a question-and-answer session in the theater lobby with a group of University of Michigan theater students. Shire tells them the show has been in preparation now for two years, and they are in Detroit "to look at the hole, not the donut." When someone asks how changes work, Maltby replies that Ockrent doesn't like to wait. "We'd go to dinner after rehearsal, and he'd say he wants a new song and new scene the next day. And we'd do it."

Back at the hotel, meanwhile, preparations are underway for ConVocation '96, a four-day symposium of mystics, magicians, astrologers and others "of a like and open mind." The opening ritual is scheduled for 7:00 p.m. tomorrow.

Thursday, February 15, 1996, Detroit

First press performance tonight. A good omen: Weidman receives word he has won the 1996 Kleban award for musical theater writing. "The next two weeks, we'll see if I deserve it," he says.

1:00 pm

Ockrent tells the cast that although nothing will change until Tuesday, the creative team is already rewriting and making structural changes to clarify the story line. Starting next week, they'll get new lines or songs after a performance, he'll rehearse the material with them the next day and it will go in that night.

"Our aim is to fix it as quickly as we can," he says. "I would like to have the show fixed musically with script and jokes, so you can get a chance to play the show and we can go in to New York fully confident."

They'd all like that, of course. But there seems to be an unlimited number of mechanical problems to sort out first. Engineer William Schmeelk is in town from Garnerville, New York, for instance, refining the shrinking machine that takes Josh back from man to boy again at the show's end.

What involved a few cuts in the film takes shape as a contraption that combines something like stilts, to which Patrick Levis' legs are strapped, with a tube that runs down his back to a piston. When he pushes a switch in his hand, the stilts should lower and the suit he is wearing simultaneously shrink. Big Josh would become little Josh once more.

Magic consultant Charles Reynolds has been in Detroit for days now, and the machine still isn't working right. The effect has to happen precisely on cue, to the second, which it does only some of the time. By the time they reach Broadway, the machine—at a cost of thousands of dollars—will be gone and the effect achieved with a simple switch of actors in darkness.

4:30 pm

Meanwhile, back at the hotel, bevies of witches have begun arriving for ConVocation '96. Participants are promised a weekend loaded with "rituals, discussions, hands-on learning and lots of drumming, dancing, singing and general celebration."

Also on the agenda are such things as "a talent show with

no gong" and "traditional folk-style songs of nature and spirit accompanied by guitar." Among the entertainers will be "some of the Pagan community's finest musicians."

Theater games begin at 9:30 p.m.

7:45 pm

In the third floor production office backstage, a monitor shows what is happening onstage. A loudspeaker broadcasts all of Zweigbaum's cues, and his voice comes over the sound system with a cue warning, a cue number or the word "go" every few seconds.

As actors head downstairs to go onstage, 25-year-old production assistant Janice Jackson looks up from her knitting and calls out to each of them, "Have a good show." Most nights she's busy adding changes to the master script in her computer, but tonight she is actually free to watch the monitor, chat with visitors and knit.

10:10 pm

Show stops. The "knife" at the base of a piece of scenery jumps out of the "dog," the hook that would otherwise attach that scenery to a cable, and the cable exits without the scenery, in this case a worktable. Moments later, stage manager Clifford Schwartz heads onstage to push the worktable across and off.

10:50 pm

Show ends to great applause. Jackson leans in close to the monitor and looks at the audience on the screen. She can't believe her eyes. "Oh, my God," she says. "They're all standing up."

Friday, February 16, 1996, Detroit

Opening night. There will be finger foods and drinks out in the lobby after the show, but the number of invited guests is going to be lower than expected. Another blizzard in New York keeps people away, including producers, friends and families of cast members.

10:00 am

Group meeting back in the bunker. Six hours. Lunch is brought in.

Creating *Big* the film was apparently quite different. Screenwriters Ross and Spielberg began with the notion of what would happen if a kid got his wish to become a grown-up. Starting to brainstorm, they turned on a tape recorder and within an hour had their entire outline. After four months of writing it on speculation, they sold it immediately to James Brooks. Although they did one major rewrite, says Ross, they did progressively smaller rewrites through production, and the script never changed in any fundamental way from that initial outline.

Ockrent and company would probably not want to know that as they tread over and over increasingly familiar ground. Returning yet again to the problematic loft scene, they worry whether the young and old Josh are consistent. Is the character that Jenkins plays the same character that Levis plays? It is, Weidman says, a discussion they've been having for three years.

On to logic. Would a kid feel uncomfortable with an adult in his room? Or would he rush around showing her stuff and getting her to play with him? Is a sexual encounter likely? Ockrent and Stroman like the notion of a "comedy of manners" between a grown woman and a 13-year-old boy who happens to look like an adult. Josh thinks one thing, Susan another. He's having a sleep-over, she's starting a relationship.

4:45 pm

Back in the theater. Choreographer Thatcher comes by with "notes" from an audience member who handed her some written comments after last night's show. Among his suggestions: put the ladies in longer skirts and add more dance numbers.

That's what happens, Ockrent says. "Next, everybody's wives, bartenders and physical therapists will suggest things."

6:00 pm

ConVocation '96 is wrapping up afternoon sessions on such topics as shields, shrines, storytelling and pendulum work. Next come dinner and book-signing.

10:00 pm

Tonight's performance disaster: Two scrollers, the devices that control the colors of light beams, go out, making loud buzzing noises. It is particularly noisy onstage where actors can barely hear themselves speak.

The controversial breast-touching scene is now a heart-touching scene, which appears to be satisfactory to producers. (Josh is back to touching Susan's breast by the time *Big* opens in New York.)

Big won't change now until at least Tuesday, since there are matinees both Saturday and Sunday this weekend, and the cast has Monday off. "It's a killer schedule," says Cypher, who played four-performance weekends as *Evita*'s Juan Peron in Los Angeles: "From the half-hour [call] on Friday to the curtain going down Sunday, you do the show five times in 49 hours. In *Evita*, I had to change clothes 35 times on matinee days. Just that is exhausting."

Ockrent isn't looking forward to those five performances either. "It's very hard to watch the show when you know scenes are changing," the director says. "It's quite unbearable."

Saturday, February 17, 1996, Detroit

Worse day yet.

The first review is out, and it isn't good. *Detroit News* critic Kenneth Jones praises the cast and choreography but says the show "still felt like a squeaky adolescent looking for a deeper voice." Weidman's book needs more comedy, Jones writes, and the score is not just thin but "created in the Land of the Generic."

This morning's production meeting results in a decision to delay New York previews and opening night. Then, at tonight's performance, part of the set crashes into another part, sending one cast member to the hospital for X-rays, the

backstage crew into a frenzy trying to get understudies dressed and onstage, and patrons stomping their feet to get the show back on.

11:30 am

About two dozen production people gather at the theater to talk about the coming Broadway run.

Production supervisor Arthur Siccardi wants to push back both previews and opening night. Even if he and his crew worked from 8 a.m. to midnight in New York, a schedule comparable to the one they've had in Detroit, they still couldn't get the show ready by April 1. Bringing in a second crew to help would be prohibitively expensive, and the Shubert Theatre renovation means that even if they closed early in Detroit, which they can't, they still couldn't get into the theater in New York any sooner.

Ockrent reviews the proposed new dates, which mean very few days onstage before performances start. "There's no time to light and rehearse on this schedule," Ockrent says with exasperation. "This is a young, inexperienced cast and a comedy, and you can't throw them onstage with no time and all that tension. It's all cutting our throats, however you look at it."

They go over the schedule again and again. How to squeeze in more previews before the opening. How to maintain the momentum of Detroit performances. How to make everything happen faster. Concludes production carpenter Olan Cottrill: "Unless we can move the earth further from the sun, we can't get another day."

Back and forth it goes for maybe an hour until they reach a series of decisions. The cast will go onstage the 4th of April, and previews will begin on the 8th. *Big* will now open not on the 25th of April but probably on April 28 or possibly even May 1, the very last day they can still qualify for this year's Tony Awards.

8:15 pm

Part of the roller coaster set crashes into an onstage car-

nival booth. Actress Jan Neuberger, who is inside that booth, feels something hit her head, is helped offstage, then taken by ambulance to the local hospital.

On a gurney in the ambulance, strapped in to keep her spine immobilized until a doctor can examine her, Neuberger is warned she'll be seeing a lot of gun and stab wounds when she gets to the hospital. (First thing she sees, however, is the metal detector that people have to go through even to get *into* the emergency room.) Neuberger has extensive X-rays, is found to be fine and sent home.

Back at the theater, meanwhile, they're rushing to both fix the set and replace Neuberger, who, in addition to several ensemble roles, is featured as Miss Watson, Josh's secretary. Corinne Melancon and dance captain Holt—the two adult "swings" hired to replace anyone but principals—were both in the top balcony, saw what happened and rushed backstage.

Last-minute understudy replacements are never easy, but these come before costumes are ready and with minimal rehearsals. Stroman and Ockrent decide to have Holt take over Neuberger's ensemble spot dancing on the piano keyboard, while Melancon takes over as Miss Watson. Since Melancon hasn't learned all the quick costume changes yet, Neuberger's "crossover" scenes are eliminated.

Wardrobe staff yank out Melancon's measurements and clothes sizes and race to put some outfits together. No wigs are ready yet either, but Neuberger's gray, shoulder-length wig seems to fit. Melancon, however, is considerably taller than Neuberger, and when she finally emerges onstage as the elegant Miss Watson, her skirt is so short it looks like a mini and the jacket so small that every time she raises her arms, a big chunk of stomach shows.

Time lost for all the changes: 22 minutes.

11:30 pm

At a meeting after the performance, technical and production staffs make plans to immediately check the sets and set changes, add another stage manager and make sure the tricky timing leaves more room for error, both human and machine.

"Every day it's something," Ockrent says in disbelief. "You wake up not knowing what will happen next. Look at what you have to go through—you get a sense of why there are so few new musicals."

Sunday, February 18, 1996, Detroit

Reviews in the *Detroit Free Press* are worse than in the *Detroit News.* Another marathon script meeting reveals that the authors of the show don't much like what they're seeing either.

11:00 am

Maltby and Shire are working in Shire's suite, where the living room table is covered with partially written music and lyrics. Maltby's computer is at one end of the table, and Shire wanders back and forth from the table to his electric keyboard to sound out potential melodies.

They're writing another song for Susan Lawrence, something called "Memo to Me" that Maltby thinks could be their 16th try at her introductory ballad. It's the sort of song the two men are famous for—contemporary women telling about their lives—but that apparently hasn't made it any easier. Nor have the reviews, all of which are piled on the coffee table.

Detroit Free Press theater critic Lawrence DeVine calls Stroman "peerless" and raves about Wagner's sets (noting Wagner "designed the fabulous moving light towers in *Dreamgirls* and most everything snazzy in New York except the Seagram's building"). Again, the score takes the most heat. DeVine says it sounded like "the aural equivalent of drafting Michael Jordan and Charles Barkley to play hockey. They have some great moves but..."

DeVine's colleague, movie writer Terry Lawson, confesses he fled at intermission "out of respect to the charming movie, to the memory of the Broadway musical as an American art form and to myself." The sets for him were "elaborately gaudy," the songs "tuneless, witless."

Shire says if they truly took it all to heart, they'd go off and become insurance salesmen. What seems to bother him most is the reviewers' depiction of the creative team as "a

bunch of crass people who cannibalized a movie and crapped all over it. They ignored how seriously we take the whole enterprise."

The composer says they have to pay attention, however. The criticism ranged from someone who respected their work, to someone who felt he and Maltby were miscast, to someone who didn't even stay for the second act.

"Everyone's work on this show alters from this moment on," Maltby says. "It's something you have to take in and adjust to. They were not charmed."

4:30 pm

Back in the bunker. Ockrent cautions everyone that the danger at this stage is random fixing: "We have to make the bits that aren't working work but keep the basic show intact."

The director outlines problem areas, addressing the book, music and choreography. He follows with a dramatic monologue, reading aloud from a very specific two-page list of changes he wants on everything from the overture to curtain calls.

Some highlights: The overture has to tell the audience they're in for an evening of magic; "It should be magical, timeless, traditional and tear at your heartstrings." The title song doesn't work. The keyboard number, "Fun," is far too long; they need to take out some of the exposition, rework the dance, cut jokes that aren't landing. Susan's first song has to show us her interior self so that when it's over we care about her. The party scene ending the first act should make better use of all the fine singers in the cast.

As for Josh, says Ockrent, they still need to come up with a reason Susan would fall for him. "We should know what on earth she sees in this guy," says the director. "Danny is a 33-year-old actor with a kid in his eyes. That's why he's Josh, and we could never find anybody else to do it."

Then there's what Ockrent calls the nobility issue. "Audiences need to see why Josh is going home again and feel that he does so having left the adult world a better place," he continues. "We have to, from the beginning, give the audience a reason why they're there."

6:15 pm

Ockrent listens to the new overture, likes what he hears and asks orchestrator Douglas Besterman if he could orchestrate the new overture tonight before heading back to New York. An astonished Gemignani turns to the equally astonished Besterman, adding, "Could you do it by 7:30, and we'll put it in the show tonight?"

It's typical Ockrent, of course, and everyone in the room knows it. He's nearly always ready to press on much faster than Maltby, Shire and Weidman, who admittedly move at what Shire calls "glacial speed." They are more talmudic, more skeptical, more inclined to hold on to scenes, songs, ideas, whatever, before letting them go.

Not Ockrent. The late George Cukor once said that if the director sits down, everyone sits down, and Ockrent obviously feels the same way. He moves quickly, his gaze continually on the big picture. A man who studied physics before turning to the theater, Ockrent likes to get everything sketched out and working, then fine tune. He mulls things over, but not for long.

7:00 pm

Ordered-in dinners have arrived and been distributed. People start eating.

7:03 pm

Ockrent notices silence. "Keep talking," he says.

Maltby gets conversation back to the troubling title song. He and Shire both feel something very damaging happened when Mrs. Baskin's first song, "Say Good Morning to Mom," was cut and the title song moved up to become the song that Josh sings immediately upon waking up as a grown-up.

"Big," the song, includes such lyrics as "It's like 'The Fly'—oh, God, it's scary/ Can't someone help me, please/ I'm not just big, I'm big and hairy/ Look, God, I'm on these knees..." The beat speeds up as Josh sings, "I don't want to be a grown-up/ How can a kid get blown up/ If I sinned, I haven't seen it/ If I said it, I don't mean it/ Put me back the way I was/ But I can't be a kid because I'm....big!!"

If they had chosen to write a song for Josh then, says Maltby, "We would not have written that song. At that moment, the show took a turn from which it could never recover. You move the wrong song to the wrong place, then try to fix it and it doesn't work anymore. The most dangerous thing in a musical is to cut something because you don't like it. Maybe it was a bad song, but with it goes a lot of stuff that is important."

Taking out Walsh's opening song helped solve some problems, Maltby tells Ockrent, but it had a "devastating" effect. "The musical we love is not happening," he says, his feelings so strong that his voice keeps breaking. "Smart people like us don't put dumb ideas into a show and derail it. Smart people like us put smart ideas into a show and derail it."

Nobody really disagrees with him at this point, including Ockrent. "The driving beat of the song is wrong for Danny's voice and for the emotion," Ockrent says. "A kid who woke up in an adult body would be horrified. We now have a main character who sings a rock and roll song as if he's just out of *Grease*."

They didn't notice it before, they figure out, because it wasn't a big rock and roll number back in the rehearsal hall when Jenkins was singing with a piano, not an orchestra. So now, they agree, they've got to fix it. "It's crucial," Ockrent says. "I don't think you're in love with Danny then and you should be."

There is a break in the conversation just then, and Jenkins' voice comes over the loudspeaker rocking and rolling his way through the title song at the evening performance.

8:05 pm

Nancy Robillard, Ockrent's assistant, bursts in to tell him they just had to bring the curtain down. The men's bathroom unit in the bus terminal scene didn't leave the stage with the rest of the set and wound up in the F.A.O. Schwarz scene.

8:15 pm

Nederlander stops by his office to tell everyone about all the calls he's getting from satisfied customers. "If this show

gets by the critics, it will run forever," he predicts. "Critics want Ibsen. But I never had people call and tell me they liked a show as much as this one. It's just like *Annie*."

Nederlander exits. "That's what he told me about *Assassins*," quips Weidman. "It's the next *Annie*."

Monday, February 19, 1996, Detroit

ConVocation '96 is over, and even the hotel maids seem relieved. Actors on their first day off are strolling the lobby with huge bags full of laundry slung over their shoulders, and it's a far more comforting sight than the strangely-clad men and women who've been wandering the halls the last four days. Wagner tells of sharing the elevator with someone in a floor-length monk's robe who was barefoot and carrying a lit candle.

Tuesday, February 20, 1996, Detroit

Item in *New York Post* that previews and opening are postponed for technical reasons. Freydberg, who is quoted extensively in the article, admits he notified the reporter. "I did it intentionally," he says. "I didn't want them to think it was because of the reviews."

If he hadn't told the press, Freydberg says, "The minute I went to the group sales people and said 'don't sell,' it would be all over the place, and everybody would think we're in trouble. And we're not. They were going to find out, and this was a good way to do it."

1:00 pm

Ockrent is already looking ahead. Changes are coming, he tells his actors. "It's why you haven't seen us. I'm not going to go through the details because a lot is in computers and the heads of Richard, David and John."

He does tell them, however, that there will be new lyrics, new choreography and some restructuring of the keyboard dance scene. From Wednesday on, there will be a lot of changes and rewrites for most of the first act. "A sexual triangle will emerge," he hints. "Ah," says Jenkins. "This will do well in France."

Today, however, there will be "adjustments" to the sec-

ond act. Among them: a scene trim means Jenkins will have 44 seconds to change from his tuxedo to his business suit. Ockrent says the costume people are "very confident" he'll be able to do it. When, a few hours later, Jenkins does actually change in 44 seconds, his colleagues applaud.

1:30 pm

Production assistant distributes the new pages, so new they're still hot from the Xerox machine. Some are read aloud before cast members disperse to learn them, rehearse with Ockrent or simply wait their turn for the next round of changes. Before they go, Ockrent closes with the reminder, "This is where it all gets fun out of town."

It's also where, as Maltby puts it, they "find the statue in the block of stone." Wagner, who compressed *A Chorus Line* down to its black velour drapes and mirrored walls, says, "Less important stuff disappears now. Lyrics have to have meaning, and it's the same with props. There are props that will disappear. When you start, you want to have everything you could possibly need. It's like having a whole refrigerator full of food. You want everything there you could possibly need, but if you used it all, it would be a bit much."

6:15 pm

Back at Il Centro restaurant. Same table. Same people. Pretty much the same food. Ockrent asks for five minutes to regroup, but he can't stay quiet that long. He thinks things went well; the cast liked the changes. Maltby and Shire report back what they've written, including what Maltby calls a new "powerhouse" melody.

Ockrent turns to Weidman: "You have that new scene for me?"

Weidman to Ockrent: "I gave you what I had this morning, and I haven't been out of your sight all day."

It is a typical exchange between the two men. If Ockrent isn't talking through the script with Weidman, suggesting lines

and bits, he's standing behind him, looking over his shoulder at what Weidman might be writing. One night at dinner, he even absent-mindedly edits some doodling that Weidman has done on the paper tablecloth.

Wednesday, February 21, 1996, Detroit

Kamlot, the general manager, is taking a fast lunch at the mall. He and his wife Jane have rented a small apartment, and he's marking off days until they head home. It isn't like being in New York where he knows how to find everything. Here he and his staff depend heavily upon the Yellow Pages. That's where they found a rehearsal studio, for instance, where dancers could rehearse on a proper wood floor rather than on a theater carpet.

Producers try to establish an environment in which creative people are able to function optimally, Kamlot explains, and his department does the same for crew members and other support personnel. Factoring in both union restrictions and human endurance, Kamlot manages people ("Who's available when?"), time ("How long can they work?") and money ("How much do we have, how much can we spend and what is it being spent for?").

Kamlot, who has managed 44 Broadway shows, including *A Chorus Line*, is given to saying things like "If you take care of the pennies, the dimes take care of themselves" and returns glass bottles to get back deposits. On *Big*, he says, "My instructions from Jim [Freydberg] were to give people what they want and need and to stay within the budget. Those are conflicting instructions."

Big's payroll includes about 75 or 80 out-of-towners who are here for more or less the entire Detroit run. Among them are not just actors but key carpenters, electricians, musicians, and wardrobe, design, light, sound and prop people. *Big* pays their plane fare to and from New York or wherever, plus per diems and, often, substantial overtime.

Another 40 to 50 copyists, designers, publicists, producers and others are here on and off to consult, but like most pre-Broadway shows, *Big* hires dozens of local musicians, dressers and others to save on per diems. "You try to hire as

many people locally as you can to run the show smoothly," says company manager Steven Chaikelson. "But the ones that travel with you from New York are the ones that you can rely on."

Now add in setting up the show and tearing it down. Says Kamlot, "Out-of-town tryouts are very expensive, and few musicals can afford them. If you can't cut costs and you can't increase ticket sales, you wind up losing money. The objective is to lose as little money as possible. [But] theater people are perennially optimistic. How can you possibly go into a venture like this without being optimistic? Would you open a business—a dress shop, a deli, a shoe store—without thinking it would be successful?"

Assistant company manager Elie Landau appears at the table. He needs Kamlot right away. Nobody else can leave the office. Would Kamlot take the van over to the rehearsal studio and pick up the children's ensemble?

Of course he will. "That's my job," he says. "Managing money, time and people."

Thursday, February 22, 1996, Detroit

Zweigbaum shows up at Ockrent's dinner table looking worried. Jon Cypher has hurt his left knee—his good knee. Before he finishes the sentence, choreographers Stroman and Thatcher are on their feet. They rush out of the restaurant, across the street and up three flights of stairs to Cypher's dressing room.

Cypher doesn't look good. He's bent over in pain and says he could hardly walk when he got off the keyboard after rehearsal. The knee brace another cast member gave him has helped, but he's still worried about the keyboard dance. Stroman and Thatcher move the flowers on the side piece in his dressing room and have him practice climbing up and down and sitting to kick. They show him how to take it easy, stepping down onto the keyboard rather than jumping, and tell him that Gemignani will slow down the tempo.

The actor decides to perform tonight, then visit an orthopedist tomorrow. Dan Jenkins, who comes by to see what's happening, says he wouldn't mind seeing the orthopedist himself.

"It's like you're a boxer in the ring," says Ockrent. "Your hands are tied behind your back, and guys come out and punch and whack you. You know they'll be back, and you don't know where they'll hit next."

The director decides to check in quickly with his writers and then head back up to watch the show. After he leaves, Shire turns to Maltby and Weidman and asks, "You guys going to be here for a while?"

Weidman replies, "Until Richard collapses. Then it will be just me."

Friday, February 23, 1996, Detroit

Announcement in today's *New York Times* that Jonathan Larson's hit musical, *Rent,* is moving from the small New York Theatre Workshop to Broadway. Opening night will be April 29, the night after *Big* opens.

11:00 am

Disturbing medical news. Cypher appears to be fine, but Jenkins is not. He went with Cypher to the orthopedist to check up on a tailbone injury and decided to ask about his left knee. It had begun to swell up lately, and he's had trouble putting weight on it.

The doctor takes a look and is not pleased with what he finds. He diagnoses a meniscus tear and recommends arthroscopic surgery. But Jenkins, who has heard that the usual rehabilitation time is six weeks or more, does not want surgery. He wants to try physical therapy instead.

1:00 pm

Rehearsal starts. They may add a new curtain call, even a new ending, Ockrent tells his cast. It depends on how far the writers get. "It's a hothouse of activity down there."

Not hot enough, apparently. By the end of the day, nobody's come up with a satisfactory way to end the show. "There has to be an elegant solution to this," Ockrent says. "You can't just drift into a curtain call. I'm virtually convinced you cannot leave after the warehouse, on a dark stage, a dark beat and a sad woman. You don't want to end your musical com-

edy there. You've got to show the world is normal again."

Eventually they will send Josh home having improved Susan's life as well as having rejoined his young friends in childhood. But not today.

7:00 pm

Dinner conversation centers on how to keep the story focused on Josh. Remember, says Maltby, "Other people walk into Josh's story. He doesn't walk into theirs." Shire considers making a sign that says, "It's about Josh, stupid."

Saturday, February 24, 1996, Detroit

Mark, who was the Twentieth Century Fox senior executive on the film *Big,* has sent Weidman a copy of the shooting draft, circling some moments and suggesting Weidman consider translating them for the stage.

"This is an adaptation, and part of that is being smart about the original and how you use it," Mark explains. "In the process of making your own piece of art, you tend to distance yourself. Right about now, you want to go back to the source material to reconnect with it and what jazzed you in the first place. Maybe there's a joke you can make use of, a character trait or a moment."

The script arrives at a time Weidman and Ockrent are again reworking scenes, and Weidman does incorporate some of Mark's suggestions. For example, Susan will now be introduced, as in the film, with a riff about how her secretary's engagement is destroying her life: "She doesn't answer my phone, she doesn't take messages. She sits at her desk all day writing her married name: Mrs. Judy Hicks. Mrs. Richard Hicks. Mrs. Judy Greenblatt-Hicks. Sometimes with a hyphen. Sometimes without a hyphen. Sometimes she *spells* the hyphen."

Sunday, February 25, 1996, Detroit

Maltby and Shire work today on a new song for the loft scene. Major inspiration, and even some of the lyrics, emerge from a long conversation with Patrick Levis, the 14-year-old boy who plays little Josh.

107

Levis, who shares a sweetness and shyness with his onstage character, is glad to tell the writers about how kids his age think: Josh is at that in-between stage where he's starting to like girls, and he's confused. He's more interested in Susan *liking* him than in her loving him.

"When a kid goes to a new school for the first time, he feels uncomfortable and all he wants is for the other kids to like him," Levis explains. "So I'm going to start thinking about things she'd like, stuff in my room. But then I realize they're boy toys, not girl toys. And the only other woman in my life is mom, and she acts differently. She's not like mom."

What emerges is the duet "Stars, Stars, Stars" (a title selected so it wouldn't be confused with the song "Stars" in *Les Misérables*). Susan's lyrics are appropriate for an adult woman, but Josh's parts of the song reflect the thinking and vocabulary of a 13-year-old boy. When Levis first heard it, "It blew me away that they put words in a song that came straight out of my mouth!"

Maltby and Shire work all day on "Stars, Stars, Stars," complete a chorus and play it for the rest of the creative team. Everyone likes it, and Ockrent wants the entire song tomorrow. When the work day is finally over, it is so late the only thing open is an all-night White Castle where Weidman, Shire and Maltby unsuccessfully attempt to eat themselves sick.

Shire, who often dines on odd-looking health foods and vitamin pills, notes that the junk food is in keeping with their spirits about now: "Stro is beating her brains out trying to figure out how to salvage 'Fun.' John has rewritten the same scenes so many times that he lost count long ago, and Richard has almost lost his voice. I'm in good health but deeply confused. Basically we all agree about what's missing and what needs to be done, but we keep running up against the same old roadblocks again and again. And we're all supposed to be smart and experienced and talented.

"I knew we had more work to do, but I couldn't have imagined we'd be in such serious trouble and get so many bad reviews."

Monday, February 26, 1996, Detroit

Review in *Variety* praises the show's sets and choreography and trashes nearly everything else. Although by this time the authors have changed *Big* so much the review is already out of date, it will be widely-read and, later, widely-quoted in New York. Its references to "the script's blatant celebration of F.A.O. Schwarz" will, among other things, set the tone for future news coverage and reviews alike.

Eyler, for one, expresses amazement. "FAO was an integral part of the show's set and choreography long before we were involved, so any criticism that we commercialized the show was inaccurate and misinformed," says the toy merchant. "The scene set at our store is also probably the most famous scene in the movie. If people went to see *Big* on Broadway and there was no dancing on the piano, I think they would be disappointed and very upset at being robbed of one of the great moments in their memory of the movie. After the movie came out, and long before *Big*, the musical, the first question people would ask when they came through our front door was 'Where's the piano?'"

Tuesday, February 27, 1996, Detroit

Two more Detroit reviews come out today, both critical of the show's score. "When we get so many reviews knocking a score that we've worked on for six years and even Mike and Susan want us to rewrite numbers we thought were sure-fire, I can't help but doubt what we're about," Shire says. "Have I totally lost my objectivity about my work?"

Wednesday, February 28, 1996, Detroit

Maltby and Shire work the entire day on one more ballad for Susan. They take it to the theater and play it for Ockrent. He responds favorably, but they can't rehearse it for two days; Moore is worried about her voice with all the new songs and wants a day off from rehearsal.

Meanwhile, Ockrent is simplifying the show. He's set aside the complicated man-to-boy shrinking machine, which now joins a previously discarded exploding rocket toy and the huge

Dr. Deathstar robot—a flying prop with 400 lights, four fog sources and eight different light voltages. The ineffectual Magic Castle is still in the show, but its days are numbered.

Thursday, February 29, 1996, Detroit

Maltby has breakthrough on lyrics for "Fun": What unites Josh, MacMillan and all the adults at F.A.O. Schwarz is they see kids playing with toys, and they want to be kids again themselves.

Josh can sing, "Fun/ You know the trick when you're small/ Fun/ A paper airplane, a ball/ Fun/ You simply have it, That's all." MacMillan can sing, "Fun/ It's what a kid seems to know/ Fun/ It's when you go with the Flow/ Fun/ It's what I had long ago." And both of them can sing, "What I wouldn't give to be/ A kid until eternity/ What I wouldn't give to be/ A kid again and have fun."

Maltby and Shire work on revisions all morning, then present their rewrite to the entire creative team and music staff at the theater. Later, when they are back at work in the bunker, the show comes in over the loud speaker. Observes Shire: "Funny how the show keeps slugging away upstairs while we sit down here rewriting it."

Friday, March 1, 1996, Detroit

New York Times On Stage, and Off column says Big producers are pushing back its opening "to accommodate some musical changes as well as the technical requirements of the show." Reporter Peter Marks calls Detroit reviews mixed, but Freydberg calls them "very promising."

Saturday, March 2, 1996, Detroit

Jenkins' knee is not getting better. His is a very physical role, and one which requires considerably more than just singing and dancing. The actor jumps on and off the piano keyboard, fights with Paul, smooches with Susan, plays basketball with the kids. He leaps onto the top bunk of a bunk bed, turning a flip on his way in. And while doing all these things, he needs to have the loose, awkward posture of a kid, not of an adult with a stiff knee.

He has begun hobbling around and realizes his knee won't get better on its own. He begins to seriously consider surgery.

Sunday, March 3, 1996, Detroit

Shire finally reads the *Variety* review and worries: "That's what the industry has read about the show up to this point." Although he and Maltby do finally finish the lyrics for "Fun"— at least for now—he is so discouraged that he admits wondering if outside writers might be brought in to help. (They aren't.)

Then things get even worse. He and Maltby play the new version of "Fun" for Stroman, Ockrent and Krane, and minor differences of opinion about the song begin to escalate. Stroman and Shire, both exhausted at this point, start snapping at each other. A bitter exchange follows, and the two part angrily. Shire, who actually winds up sobbing in the corridor of the Fisher Building, realizes the *Variety* review "did get to me."

Monday, March 4, 1996, Detroit

Shire, Stroman and Krane meet at the theater at noon. Nobody refers to the night before; no apologies are made. They smile, shake hands and get back to work.

Last night, Stroman and Krane worked on dance arrangements for the new melody, and now she is rechoreographing the number. "A dance arrangement is a variation on the original melody, and our old dance arrangement no longer applied because the melody was different," she explains. "We had to toss it out and start over."

But that is not all she is doing. Because New York director Steve Horn is in town for the day shooting the show's television commercial, Stroman is choreographing dances for the commercial onstage, then rushing out during breaks to rechoreograph "Fun" in the lobby. Her dance team is helping her, as are the two young stand-bys, Medeiros and Pickler, who are not in the commercial. By the end of the day, she is nearly done.

Wednesday, March 6, 1996, Detroit

Rehearsals start on the revised "Fun."

111

Stroman rehearses the kids today and will rehearse the adults tomorrow. Given their performances each evening, days are long. But Stroman finds the cast receptive. "Not only did the melody change, but the lyrics also changed and became pertinent to the plot," she says. "There was a great sense of relief and enjoyment that they were getting a new number that would make a major difference. Which it did."

The choreographer is feeling a great deal of pressure to get the number into the show fast. It is the last week in Detroit, and she wants to know whether or not it will work onstage before they get back to New York.

Adding to the pressure, of course, is the increasing probability their leading man will have knee surgery. Ockrent now assumes that without surgery Jenkins' knee will get worse, and he won't be able to do the show at all. And if he postpones it, there is no guarantee his leg will hold up.

Greenblatt, who had arthroscopic surgery himself, suggests his own doctor, but that doctor is unavailable. Another surgeon is found, and Jenkins' operation is scheduled for next week in New York.

Observes Cypher: "A $10 million production is hanging by a meniscus."

Thursday, March 7, 1996, Detroit

Susan's newest song, "Here We Go Again," goes in tonight. Moore got the song last night after the show, then went up to the second floor of the theater to learn it while they were turning out the house lights. "Less than 24 hours later," says Moore, "I was alone, in the spotlight, singing a song I knew I didn't really know. I was living the actor's nightmare."

As insurance onstage, she put her lyrics on top of a file folder she was carrying, "but since it was such a pattery song, it didn't help. You don't know where the problem will be, and by the time you look down, it's too late."

This has happened before, of course. Moore recalls a time when lyrics for "I'll Think About it Later," the song she had when they left New York, changed on the stairs between the first and second floors of the Fisher Theater. "Another time, Richard Maltby called me," she says, "asking if I'd learned

the song yet. When I said no, he said, 'Good, because I changed it.'

"A certain amount of it is a challenge. You get faster and faster at doing it. You go back and forth between feeling despondent and overwhelmed, thinking it's a challenge, rising to it and growing from it even."

Friday, March 8, 1996, Detroit

Last rehearsal prior to closing weekend. It's three degrees out, there's a wind chill factor way below zero, but no locusts yet.

Like Moore, the rest of the cast has to adapt to changed lines, songs and dance steps. Actors tape new lines to props and hope other actors are prepared. "You wonder, 'Does the guy I'm coming at like a freight train know *his* lines?'" says Cypher. "And do we both remember we're on the same page of the rewrite of the rewrite?"

The result is short fuses, and everyone reports constant bickering. Thatcher sometimes feels that she ought "to put on goggles and a helmet to give people notes," and actors admit they're more irritable. A few days ago, lighting designer Paul Gallo and Freydberg argued about having the crew work overnight so that Gallo could light again early in the morning, something that would require considerable overtime. Push came to shove, and Ockrent finally had to break the thing up.

"There's so much at stake and look what's happening," Greenblatt says of the continuing altercations. "This is like a good marriage. But instead of two people, it's a lot of people. There will be breakthroughs, but you're going to be stepping on each other's toes. Everyone is in everyone else's head all the time."

2:45 pm

Ockrent is in Shire's hotel suite. Shire is at the piano, Maltby at the table, Weidman on the sofa. As Maltby sings "Welcome to MacMillan Toys," a perky, upbeat song about making toys, Ockrent looks more and more glum. "It feels retrograde," he says. "We're digging up something from two years ago from your trunk."

He isn't joking. The song has indeed been resuscitated, and Ockrent, always the gracious Englishman, is giving it this last shot. But what will be happening onstage during this song, which sounds to him like it came straight out of *How to Succeed in Business Without Really Trying*? And how will they be able to get 30 people offstage fast enough?

The director looks truly depressed. Though they've finally solved the problem of Susan's ballad, now the rest of the office scene is a mess. It comes 40 minutes into the show and is loaded with plot needs: the scene brings in new characters, introduces the toy company, sets up Susan's reasons for going to Josh's loft and more. They are, he groans, "in musical hell."

5:25 pm

Back at the theater, Stroman is rehearsing a new rock and roll chunk of "Fun." "Shake those legs," she calls out. "Shake them like MC Hammer or James Brown."

That includes the dancing bear. Vlastnik, who is also Jenkins' understudy, was originally supposed to be onstage as Truffles the Teddy Bear for the entire scene at F.A.O. Schwarz, then suddenly spring to life when Moore fell on him. The fall was cut and, fortunately for the guy trapped in a hot furry costume, the bear's onstage time decreased. But for every performance here (and, later, in New York) Vlastnik still needs at least five minutes and two helpers to climb into the heavy, cumbersome costume.

He snared the bear role during rehearsals. "We were getting ready to do the scene, and we knew somebody was going to be the bear," says Vlastnik. "Mike gave me a very bemused look, and I knew I was the chosen one."

11:15 pm

There are nearly a dozen cast members scrunched into Vlastnik's hotel room for one of his "video nights." Among the actor's video highlights are bloopers at awards shows, terrible dance numbers by famous people who can't dance and songs by stars who can't sing—what Vlastnik calls "Bad award show moments and people generally embarrassing themselves."

114

Video nights vary. "We watch good things, too," he says. "We're not cruel people. But some nights we just need a laugh."

Saturday, March 9, 1996, Detroit
12:00 noon

Ockrent has put together another two-page memo summarizing all the things about the show that make him crazy. Generally, he's still frustrated that they're not getting inside Josh's head the way they've finally gotten inside Susan's; isn't there a way to make us care more about this guy? Ockrent's very specific "to do" list covers everything from rewriting the opening scene and title song to writing a whole new song and dance number to end the first act.

But first there's this meeting with Wagner about the set. At the conference table in the bunker, Ockrent and Wagner review their notes as producers, writers and others wander in and out. The set, like everything else, will be adjusted for Broadway and for a stage that will be deeper but narrower than Detroit's Fisher. Some pieces will have to be cut down, others refurbished or repaired.

It's another chance to make changes. Wagner will redesign graphics in the mall scene, for instance; signs will be parodies of fast-food chains rather than the real thing. Ockrent thinks that will be both funnier and less distracting. (Local critics had assumed that signs for McDonald's, Burger King and others meant paid advertising on stage; Freydberg says that was not the case, although he hasn't ruled it out for future touring productions.) But in order to recycle existing signs, the designer will keep the new names and logos similar to the old ones. Wendy's will become Mendy's; Au Bon Pain will become Au Croissant.

The conversation gets around to "Fun," and Wagner compares the keyboard in *Big* to the dancing printing press in *Crazy for You* that disappeared during that show's pre-Broadway tryout. Like it, the keyboard is a great prop but a choreographer's nemesis. "I think you're stopped by the piano," Wagner tells Ockrent. "It limits what you can do with the dancers."

115

Wagner, not shy about expressing himself, has opinions on everything and punctuates the set discussion with comments on songs, scenes, motivation and structure. Where's the finality between Susan and Josh? How come Josh is so confident the first time he's alone with her? As Wagner goes on, Ockrent first folds his arms across his chest, then moves his chair back from the table.

Wagner, undeterred, starts making suggestions for the troublesome ending of the show. Finally, exasperated, Ockrent turns to Wagner: "You've been away. We tried everything. We even had a curtain call in the neighborhood [instead of at F.A.O. Schwarz]." Then, standing, Ockrent walks across the room. "Meeting adjourned," he says, opening the door.

1:15 pm

Producers Mark and Greenblatt understand Ockrent's frustration, they say over soup at the mall. The movie could end with a nice coda of Josh and Billy back as kids, wheeling their bikes up a street. "In a movie, it's a cut," says Mark, who has been involved in producing such films as *Black Widow* and *Working Girl*. "Here, it's a logistical nightmare."

The reviews have also taken their toll, Greenblatt says, calling them "startling" to everyone. "We all thought the show was in better shape than it really was," he says. "Now it gets real serious. When you're losing by 20 points and it's the first quarter, it doesn't much matter. But if you're down by six points with 30 seconds left to play, it becomes critical. We don't have time for a lot of mis-shots now. Trial and error time is over."

3:50 pm

Matinee crisis: During a big production number in the second act, a ladies' compact goes flying across the stage, scattering powder everywhere and turning the place into sort of an ice rink. One actor falls, others slide into one another, and somebody even adds, "Watch out!" to her section of the song. In the next scene, which includes an onstage kitchen, three actresses ad lib a housekeeping moment as they get down on their hands and knees to try to clean up the mess.

Shire compares what's going on to a heart transplant with

the patient still awake.

11:15 pm

Post-performance party in the hotel's ballroom tonight to celebrate the end of the Detroit run. Kids go out on the dance floor and improvise a line dance. F.A.O. Schwarz executive Eyler, his wife Dolores and 13-year-old son Todd are sitting it out, although Todd clearly wants to get up and dance, too. ("I know how he felt," his father says later. "It would be sort of like going out and playing golf with Arnold Palmer.") When Maltby spots Todd in all his eagerness, he alerts Ockrent, and soon some of the teenage girls in the show get young Eyler out on the dance floor.

Suddenly, the end of the first act comes into focus. "We had been looking for a way for Josh to take the lead, and teaching executives a dance was too knowing," says Maltby. "But Josh, having been to bar mitzvahs in New Jersey, would know line dances. It would not be a difficult leap for him to make use of the presence of kids and get the grown-ups to do the same dance, because it happens at every bar mitzvah."

Maltby, in fact, had been thinking about line dances himself since he attended a bat mitzvah in New Jersey three years earlier. "Rock dancing is usually disorganized, but here is a kind of rock dancing that is organized. Kids come together and look like they've been choreographed. It's completely in their vocabulary. We had all talked about line dancing many times, but it never before had a place in the show."

Now it will.

Sunday, March 10, 1996, Detroit

Last two Detroit performances. Cast and crew are buying up souvenirs at the stand in the lobby.

People are really eager to leave. A brawl last night in the hallway across from Freydberg's hotel room left the producer unable to open his front door this morning. A few miles away, some of the musicians arrived home to find a shooting victim on the ground out front. Then today, Brett Tabisel and Enrico Rodriguez were at the money machine in the deserted mall adjacent to the hotel when three menacing guys started to en-

117

circle them. The boys turned and ran as fast as they could. Says Tabisel: "I can't wait to get back to New York where it's safe."

2:00 pm

Matinee begins. Ockrent can't stand to watch the show anymore, knowing how much it will change, so he's down in the bunker. Looking ahead to New York, he decides that when the cast starts rehearsing there on Thursday, he'll first polish the existing show, then add in new material the following week. But he isn't telling the creative team his plan. It's better they think he expects their revisions on Thursday; they'll work faster.

3:50 pm

Intermission. Weidman appears in the bunker.
Ockrent: "How did the office scene look?"
Weidman: "Pretty good."
Ockrent: "Pretty good?"
Weidman: "At least I wasn't ducking behind the ushers in fear I would be recognized."
Ockrent looks at his watch. Their plane doesn't leave for a couple hours, meaning there's still time to talk through a little dialogue, some possible lyrics. Ockrent suggests Weidman scribble down a few phrases Josh might sing in a new song for the end of the first act. Weidman can do it on the plane.

4:20 pm

Knock at the door. Shire comes in, looking excited. He sings a few bars of new music for the top of the show, and, he says, he and Maltby just may have a song to end the first act. Stroman and Shire start talking about the line dancing the kids did at the party the night before. Maybe it will work well onstage. It wouldn't be "here comes the big song" either, Shire says; it could emerge from the scene.

Ockrent reads aloud from a newspaper interview in which he is quoted as saying, "I've learned I ought to get out of this business. I ought to try something simple—like brain surgery." He laughs uncontrollably.

4:45 pm

Matinee ends to warm applause. "We're going out with a better reaction than when we came in," the director says before heading backstage, then out to the airport and home. "That's always a good sign."

10:15 pm

Final performance ends. No glitches. Curtain comes down after a standing ovation, and within 10 minutes of the show's end, a stage manager rips Dan Jenkins' name off his dressing room door. Supper is laid out in the carpentry shop for the dozens of people who will work all night "striking" the show.

Monday, March 11, 1996, Detroit

Overnight crew grows to 60 by 4:00 a.m. Sets are coming down, trucks are loading up; plans call for unloading at the Shubert Theatre in New York around 8:00 Tuesday morning. "Now we're going to do the whole thing over," says Kamlot, "and, hopefully, with some prior knowledge, quicker and more efficiently."

Shows move like circuses, bundling and unbundling their goods in town after town. Often, the packaging has come from earlier circuses: two *Big* wig storage boxes, for instance, still have *La Cage aux Folles* signage on them. And when *Big* becomes history, its two $750 "wig oven" hair dryers will go the same route, sold to the highest bidder.

Departing theater tenants make deals as well. *Big* was able to buy $2,200 of costume items from *Crazy for You*, saving on retail costs of such things as hanging racks, garment bags, desks, iron cleaners, body pads, irons, sleeve boards, and spot removers. To build just two new lighting platforms of fireproof lumber would have run upwards of $20,000, estimates Kamlot, who was able to get the platforms and other equipment for $4,000. Everybody made out on that deal, he thinks.

Bottom line from Freydberg: It cost $2 million to try out in Detroit, plus running losses of "a little over $200,000." Had

119

they tried out the show in Boston last summer as planned, he says, it would also have cost $2 million. But since they would have played Boston without a subscription base, additional running losses could have been between $1 and $1.5 million.

The magical Zoltar grants hero Josh Baskin's wish to be big, launching a film, a musical and a line of toys. Costume design sketch courtesy of William Ivey Long.

Patrick Levis, as Josh, makes his wish to be big.

Daniel Jenkins plays adult Josh. Asked about taking on what became a signature role for the much-loved Tom Hanks, Jenkins says: "It's a rather warm shadow to be standing in."

Photos: Joan Marcus/Carol Rosegg

Big rehearses at 890 Broadway, the Flatiron District building where many musicals take shape.

At piano, musical director Paul Gemignani tries a melody as director Mike Ockrent and choreographer Susan Stroman listen intently.

Media attention to the show was unrelenting in both New York and Detroit.

Photos: Barbara Isenberg

Rehearsals continue at 890 Broadway prior to the pre-Broadway tryout in Detroit.

Playwright John Weidman, here with Ockrent and Stroman, wrote many new phrases, lines and scenes both before and after the Detroit tryout.

Choreographer Stroman works with *Big* kids on one of the many numbers they dance in the show.
Photos: Patricia Decker

Eleven of the *Big* cast members are under 15. Number auditioned for those 11 parts: 800.

Here they are in the rehearsal hall, being kids.

Photo: Barbara Isenberg

And onstage, being actors.

Photo: Joan Marcus/ Carol Rosegg

Big sets include offices, houses, the New York Port Authority, F.A.O. Schwarz and more.

A New Jersey neighborhood. Set designer Robin Wagner says he wanted to use simple geometric shapes which would reflect the world as a child sees it.

Wagner's carnival set for Wild Thunder, the roller coaster that Josh wished to be big enough to try. The ride also came to symbolize the show itself for many of its principals.

Courtesy: Robin Wagner studio

Cast and crew set off for Detroit and six long weeks trying out their show before its Broadway opening.

Photo: T. L. Boston

In Detroit, writers often work in theater operator Joseph Nederlander's windowless office, a place so depressing it came to be known as "the bunker."

Librettist John Weidman writes.

And director Mike Ockrent concludes another six-hour script meeting.

Photos: Barbara Isenberg

Songs appeared and disappeared during the show's Detroit tryout. Songwriting team of Richard Maltby, Jr., and David Shire eventually wrote 58 songs for *Big*.

Composer Shire at piano in lobby of Detroit's Fisher Theatre.

Shire and Maltby work in Shire's suite at Detroit's St. Regis Hotel. Their songs and shows date back to their first meeting at Yale 40 years ago.

Photos: Barbara Isenberg

High spirits onstage despite the chilly reviews as

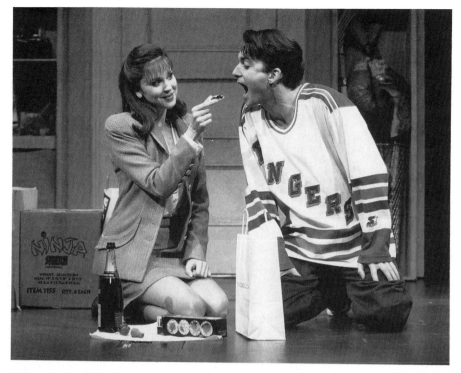

Crista Moore offers Daniel Jenkins some caviar, then does a quick sidestep to avoid his childlike reaction to a mouth full of fish eggs.

Jenkins, atop his boss's desk, is king of the grownups in a second act production number.

Photos: Joan Marcus/ Carol Rosegg

Other members of *Big* cast include:

Jon Cypher plays toy company executive MacMillan.

Barbara Walsh performs as Josh's mother, Mrs. Baskin.

Ensemble member Frank Vlastnik's many parts include dancing as Truffles the Teddy Bear.

Photos: Barbara Isenberg (above), Joan Marcus/Carol Rosegg (right)

Big's opening night party is held at co-producer F.A.O. Schwarz's Fifth Avenue store, where stars Brett Tabisel, Daniel Jenkins, Crista Moore and Jon Cypher (left to right) pause to demonstrate the dance-on piano in the toy store's *Big* shop.

Publicist Chris Boneau, producer James Freydberg, choreographer Susan Stroman and director Mike Ockrent (left to right) read the *New York Times* review during the opening night party. Wrote critic Vincent Canby: "It worked as a movie. It works as a show."

Photo: T.L. Boston

Recording session for the *Big* original cast album is held on May 6, the same day that Tony nominations are announced.

Cast album is produced by multi-Grammy winner Phil Ramone (center), here with Maltby and Shire.

Brett Tabisel, who earlier was nominated for Drama Desk award, today also received Tony nomination for his portrayal of Josh's best friend, Billy.

Dan Jenkins

The kids from *Big*

Photos: Joan Marcus/Carol Rosegg

Big received 5 Tony nominations—including for book, score and choreography—but was not nominated for Best Musical. Neither was *Victor/Victoria*. *New York Post* front page for May 7 comments on the Tony nominations.

Ex-employees sue Leona for $100M — Page 7 — *Helmsley*

Heavy drinking and hot groping before cop's arrest — Page 18 — *Robinson*

NEW YORK POST

HOME DELIVERY
1-800-940-7678
CALL TODAY!

LATE CITY FINAL

TUESDAY, MAY 7, 1996 / Mostly sunny today, high around 60; cloudy tonight, 40-45 / Details, Page 26 ★★   · 50¢

Furor as 'Victor/Victoria,'
'BIG' are overlooked
for top musical award

TONY BALONEY

Julie Andrews, star of "Victor/Victoria," garnered the only Tony nomination for the hit musical.

Full coverage: Pages 4, 5 & 41

Plan to cut sales tax on clothes will die in Albany: Page 6

Big settles into Broadway's newly-renovated Shubert Theatre, ending its long odyssey from hit film to stage musical.

Photo: T.L. Boston

PART FOUR:
BROADWAY

"If I was on a B17, returning to London from a bombing run over Berlin, and we had lost three engines and the compass, and there was a hole in the fuel tank, the one person I'd want to be the pilot would be Mike Ockrent."
—Robin Wagner to James B. Freydberg
Somewhere over America between Detroit and New York,
March 9, 1996

Wʜᴇɴ *Big* moves into the Shubert Theatre on April 4, it is hardly recognizable. One-third of the score has been changed, the title song is gone, a new production number closes the first act and there's a new ending.

Rewriting continues in New York, first in the rehearsal hall and later onstage as well. Most rehearsals start with lists of script changes. Usually they are what Maltby calls "fixing, cleaning and polishing tiny moments"—a phrase here, a line there—but sometimes they involve whole new stanzas for songs.

Weidman, Maltby and Shire are generally in the foyer of the lower lobby ladies room, a place with a couple of side tables, chairs and sofa. It is rare during the day to find them away, and even when they are, they usually leave behind computers, printers, yellow legal pads. Robillard, whom Ockrent sometimes introduces as his aide-de-camp, is continually running up and down the stairs with new pages for Ockrent to see.

Always on their minds now are the critics, the people Mark calls "that New York sophisticated gang." Bad buzz from Detroit seems to have eased, but what happened there could happen here as well. "We thought we had something good going into Detroit," says Greenblatt. "I asked Stro how so many of us could be wrong, and she said that until you have the show onstage, you just don't know. We feel sure again now, but until we're back onstage, nobody knows."

The Shubert, flagship of the legendary theater chain, has been completely renovated. Now *Big* must live up to its predecessors, *A Chorus Line* and *Crazy for You*. If it doesn't, Andrew Lloyd Webber is reportedly waiting in the wings with his newest show, *Whistle Down the Wind*.

Wednesday, March 13, 1996

Jenkins is at New York University Hospital having pre-

surgery lab tests. Ockrent and Freydberg aren't feeling so hot themselves.

When Jenkins first called Ockrent, says the director, "I anticipated disaster."

With surgery set for tomorrow, Ockrent continues to imagine the worst. Nobody knows how the operation will turn out, and neither Ockrent nor Freydberg wants an understudy to do the first preview.

The two men review their options. They consider not only postponing previews but even cancelling the opening and missing the Tony deadline of May 1.

As insurance, they decide to quietly take tickets off sale for the first three performances. "I am not going to do a first preview in New York without Dan," Ockrent declares.

Ockrent doesn't tell the cast or even the writers that he is prepared to postpone. "We didn't want to tell them and take the pressure off," he says later.

Thursday, March 14, 1996

First day of rehearsal back in New York. Everyone looks healthier and happier than in Detroit. Fresh air and sunlight don't hurt, notes actress Joan Barber. "When you're on the road, you have to be a hunter and a gatherer," adds colleague Donna Lee Marshall, who saw the world with *Cats*. "You don't even notice the stress until you're back home and realize it isn't there anymore."

Missing from the rehearsal hall, however, is leading man Jenkins. He's over at the hospital having arthroscopic surgery. Outpatient procedure.

Jenkins is told he'll be able to go back to work fairly shortly, using crutches so he doesn't put weight on his knee or limp. "What I worried about was how quickly my body would heal," he says later. "I was worried about letting people down."

Sunday, March 17, 1996

New York Times Arts & Leisure section devotes front page and several inside pages to "the birth of a theatrical comet"— *Rent.*

The *Times* spread is merely the latest in an extraordinary outpouring of local and national reviews, features, commentary and other coverage of the highly-acclaimed musical.

A rock opera inspired by Puccini's *La Bohème, Rent* was immediately recognized as a theatrical breakthrough after its Off Broadway opening last month at the small New York Theatre Workshop. When its 35-year-old creator, Jonathan Larson, died unexpectedly of an aortic aneurism just hours after the show's final dress rehearsal, it added human tragedy to the story of Larson's achievement. Few tales have been so well documented, so well reported.

Larson's bohemians are denizens of the East Village, young people addicted to drugs as well as to art, and his story is one of love and triumph amid illness, poverty and misunderstanding. His powerful score is sung by a talented but previously unknown cast, many of whom skyrocket to acclaim along with the show.

By the time *Rent* opens on Broadway on April 29, Larson will already have received, posthumously, the 1996 Pulitzer Prize for drama.

Monday, March 18, 1996

Tickets go on sale today at Shubert box office and at F.A.O. Schwarz.

Back in the rehearsal hall, Ockrent has been experimenting with a new ending. The kids' ensemble appears more often throughout the show now, and Ockrent is currently weaving the kids into the closing warehouse scene. They go with Josh and Billy to find that elusive Zoltar machine as sort of an adventure. Josh's farewell to Susan and return to his mom are nestled in a livelier, less downbeat setting. Add a nice surprise spin and, finally, *Big* has its ending.

At around 5:00 p.m., several of the actors, Gemignani, Ockrent and others head uptown to Jenkins' apartment on the Upper West Side. There's food on the kitchen table, chairs set up in the living room and worry on everyone's faces.

The good news is that the title song has at last been replaced. Josh now sings "This Isn't Me," sometimes called "the song formerly known as 'Big.'" It is slower than its predeces-

sor and focuses on Josh's astonishment at what has happened to his body: "What's this foot?/ I know my foot/ And this is not my foot/ This isn't me/ I'm too tall to fit my bunk/ And my favorite shirt has shrunk/ What I'm looking at is gross/ This isn't me!"

In his cozy living room, surrounded by his colleagues, a seated Jenkins tries the lyric for the first time as his 16-month-old son, Jack, screams along. The actor's crutches are leaning against the piano, and somebody asks Ockrent when his leading man will be able to get around without them. "I don't know," he replies, almost inaudibly. "Danny doesn't know. The doctors won't even know for a week."

Tuesday, March 19, 1996

Stroman and Ockrent are rehearsing the final scene of the first act, now rewritten to bring on the kids as well as the adults. The office party has become a family event, incorporating a large production number that Maltby and Shire are working on in the tiny studio next door.

Late in the afternoon, Stroman leaves the main room to check on their progress. Shire is at the piano, and Maltby is lying on a table along one wall, his arm draped on the piano top. Stroman scrunches in the corner as Shire plays a rousing, rhythmic piece with a heavy beat. Maltby sings it out, his leg beating time on the tabletop.

When they're done, Stroman inhales, smiles, compliments them, then adds that it seems slower than the last version. They tell her not to worry. The songwriters have one more, which they play next. Stroman likes it better.

Back in the rehearsal hall, Jenkins has become participant and observer simultaneously. He sits off to one side, his leg usually elevated. Holt is standing in for him, physically acting out Josh's role. But Holt is silent; from his chair about 10 feet away, Jenkins says his lines. The actor also enjoys commenting on the action, and Ockrent sometimes feels he's got another director in the house; he stages something, and Jenkins leans over and says, "I don't know. Do you think that's funny?"

Not a great time for press coverage, but Ockrent decides

against postponing today's scheduled visit from *New York Times* reporter Peter Marks. Marks will later write a pre-opening feature about *Big*, but in the meantime Jenkins co-stars as an item in Marks' Friday column on Broadway, the boulevard of broken bones.

Wednesday, March 20, 1996

Meeting at Serino Coyne to discuss media buys.

Big is already overshadowed by press attention lavished upon both *Rent* and *Bring in 'da Noise, Bring in 'da Funk*, and Freydberg knows that all this hype can affect *Big* in terms of Tony consideration as well as audience interest. Both shows plan sizeable print advertising campaigns, capitalizing on the excellent reviews they received Off Broadway. Since Freydberg can't do that, he's adopted a new promotional strategy: small newspaper ads and large television buys. "You have two shows coming to Broadway with reviews and quotes," says the producer. "All we can do to compete is to stay out of the papers and show them the show."

Under discussion today is the best way to do that—which television shows to buy and when to buy them. Larry Miller, whose firm Corinthian is one of Serino Coyne's media buyers, prefers reaching fewer people more often. Remember what we all learned in school about the learning curve, Miller says: "The quicker you enforce it, the more they remember it."

They decide on morning shows, late news and shows preceding prime time programming, all cheaper than prime time and better pegged to their ticket-buying audience. A likely prospect—and one they eventually do pursue—is an expensive but well-targeted local buy during the Academy Awards extravaganza.

Feld put up an additional $500,000 for television advertising during this pre-opening period, Freydberg says later, bringing their marketing budget up to an impressive $1.3 million. "What we've done is get the word out," Freydberg says. "Once previews start, if word-of-mouth is good, we'll really take off.

"Now we have the emotional roller coaster. Will we be a hit or won't we?"

Thursday, March 21, 1996

Maltby and Shire have been writing and rewriting "Cross the Line" for days now. Even when it was too slow, the song worked as a line dance and Stroman could choreograph it. After just one morning, Maltby says admiringly, the whole company had learned it. But when Stroman decided that her dance required a faster tempo, they essentially had to start over again.

Asked what tempo might be right, Stroman suggested that of the Supremes' "You Can't Hurry Love," which didn't yield a good song. The songwriters asked for another, and she suggested Billy Joel's "Tell Her About It," which has the same tempo but a different feel. Although that seemed better, they left Ockrent's apartment last night without their song.

This morning, Maltby heads out early for Shire's home in Snedens Landing. There, for a change, the two men work in the living room instead of in Shire's studio. Around 11:00, they play the Billy Joel song for tempo, and Shire starts to improvise. Maltby yells, "What's that? Keep that."

They are done in half an hour.

Friday, March 22, 1996

The chorus is now written for "Cross the Line." Maltby is at his computer trying to finish the rest of the lyrics and starts typing out what Josh might think if he got kissed.

"I wrote this list of things—he'd feel scared, excited, jazzed up, really good, really weird—and I stopped and looked at the computer," says Maltby. "I'd written, 'I feel tall, I feel grown, I feel big.' I thought, 'Oh, my God.' We never personalized it before. Up until this moment, he felt like a boy in this freakish body. But the kiss makes him feel grown up, big for the first time, and that's what the show is about."

Maltby is so staggered by what's on his computer screen, he doesn't trust it. Too easy. Too obvious to have this moment happen right in front of you 30 seconds before the curtain goes down. He calls Weidman and asks if it seems right. Weidman says yes, Maltby finishes it and within a week, the song is up and staged.

130

"It was both by design and a miracle," Maltby says later. "There it was and I asked, 'Who wrote it?' It has to have been me. I always say I don't have a memory of writing songs, and that's a perfect example. I'm inside the character and the scene, and suddenly the right choice is there.

"It's the most collaborative choice in the whole show. Mike defined that children had to be there. I was sure we had to hear from Josh because of the white suit. John worked out the idea of the kids coming to the party and how the lines would be drawn between the two sides. Stro had the dance almost done before we had the right song, and we wrote the song to the dance she had already choreographed. We had tried to find it for two years, and it always seemed forced. This seemed completely organic."

Saturday, March 23, 1996

Ockrent and Weidman meet at F.A.O. Schwarz this morning. They are stuck on the "Fun" production number set in the store and opt for some on-site research. The two men happen upon a boy holding up a floor display of battery-operated toy animals attached to balloons. (The store attaches the balloons since the toys are so small that people might otherwise trip over them.) The image is precisely what they have been looking for, and Weidman heads home to write the toy into his script.

"We were really getting nowhere," says Ockrent, "and it was an exciting little morning for us. It was art imitating life."

Afternoon isn't bad either. Back in the rehearsal hall, the cast learns the new "Cross the Line" lyrics and reviews dance steps. The number is blocked by the end of the day, and among the people on hand for the late afternoon run-through are both Eyler and son Todd. Ockrent tells Eyler that it was watching Todd "cross the line" back in Detroit that helped shape the dance number.

Friday, March 29, 1996

Jenkins is moving around now and invites his physical therapist to today's run-through. During the piano keyboard

number, she flings her hands to her face, an image straight out of Edvard Munch's "The Scream" (or the movie *Home Alone*).

Sunday, March 31, 1996

"We're all hopeful again," says Shire, "but it's a question of whether we cross the magic threshold. You can get all the pieces working great, but until you get it put together in front of an audience, you can't be sure of that wonderful musical comedy synergy where everything's greater than the sum of its parts."

Monday, April 1, 1996

Big shops start opening today in all 37 F.A.O. Schwarz stores nationwide.

Here at home, the toy store's 58th St. windows are glass-enclosed billboards for *Big*, and so are the front door and the windows on 5th Avenue. Inside the store, the escalator deadends at the *Big* sales center, with its costumed ticket-seller, giant dance-on piano, and show-related products. The *Big* television commercial plays continuously on a monitor just inside the front door.

FAO has worked closely with Feld's circus companies in developing a product line. Marlene Voelker, director of product development for Feld, watched the film *Big* several times for inspiration and drew on the expertise of her eight-year-old daughter, Shara. The musical itself inspires such items as Zoltar notebooks, denim jackets, and planetariums that project stars on the ceiling. FAO had plans to develop inflatable Magic Castle toys, but dropped them when the prop was cut from the show.

Big's design team is still pulling potential props from FAO shelves. Toys that look too good for MacMillan Toys, a company in trouble, are replaced by others that can be dumbed-down by the design staff. Property master William Sweeney guesses there are now between 400 and 500 props in the show. But more than 200 stuffed animals and toys have already been discarded and sent on to toy heaven.

Tuesday, April 2, 1996

Peter Marks' article about the show is in today's *New York Times*. He touches on some of the problems and reports the poor reception in Detroit. Maltby is quoted as saying he feels the theater community is both building them up and waiting for them to fall.

It's the last day at 890 Broadway, and cast members say they hope Ockrent plans only a few more cuts and rewrites. "There have been so many versions of things, it's hard to get clear and launch a scene fresh," Moore admits. "It's confusing, and the more tired you get, the harder it is to be creative. It's like a creative obstacle course."

Weidman, Maltby and company aren't done with her yet, however. They're polishing up that new song for her at the end of the first act and thinking about a change or two in an earlier ballad. Among the decisions Maltby has yet to make: "Should it be 'he does not know me' or 'you do not know me?'" (He chooses the former.)

Stroman says Maltby, Shire and Weidman follow her and Ockrent home every night. Maltby and Weidman even laugh at themselves about all the rewrite sessions. Their working lunches would number in the teens now, says Maltby, "but if you distilled from that what ideas actually went into the show, even temporarily, it would be three peas and a string bean." Adds Weidman: "And we're not sure about the string bean."

Wednesday, April 3, 1996

Cast gets a day off and newly-renovated Shubert hosts a party.

Pianist Patrick Brady, a member of *Big*'s music team, is playing songs from *A Chorus Line*, *Crazy for You*, *Big* and other shows as guests file into the 83-year-old Shubert to celebrate its $3.7 million restoration. Stephen Sondheim is master of ceremonies for a crowd of producers, celebrities and assorted craftspeople who worked on the massive redo. Stairwells up to the balcony still smell of paint as guests take their seats.

New York Mayor Rudolph Giuliani declares today Sam S. Shubert Day, presenting a proclamation to Shubert executives Bernard Jacobs and Gerald Schoenfeld. The mayor reminds his audience that Broadway is the city's biggest tourist attraction.

Speaker Freydberg says that every producer's dream is to audition a show for the Shuberts and have them want it. "And," concludes Freydberg, "we're hoping that when we close, the next restoration will have to happen."

Thursday, April 4, 1996

First rehearsal onstage. Workmen are drilling at the back of the theater, seats aren't numbered yet, and there's still no paint on the walls upstairs. As the cast drifts in, Jan Neuberger is asked how she is. She smiles. "This is the Shubert Theatre—the shrine of show business. I feel great."

So does Ockrent. "If you've been here before, welcome back to Broadway," he tells his players. "If you're a first-timer, welcome to Broadway."

Forget Detroit, he suggests. "We're going to be here a long time...at least double the length of *Crazy for You*."

Meanwhile, there are some things they should know about the Shubert. Because the distance from the stage to the back of the house is short, the theater is very intimate. "They can see your eyes," the director says. "You have to always be in the scene and concentrated."

At least no one has to worry so much about cable and set snafus. "Everything until now has been adjusted to where they were performing," explains Wagner. "Now the sets are in the theater they were designed for. If they don't look good here, we have no excuse."

They do look good, in part because they've been spiffed up since Detroit. For instance, the New Jersey backdrop is now three-dimensional, something Wagner says he was denied earlier because of budget cuts. Improving the backdrop has added several thousand dollars to the show's costs.

Kamlot seems to have given up on budget control. "When the production first started, it was like a train going at 55

jams. Same problem as Detroit. A crew member is onstage, flat on his belly, with a flashlight, looking under the unit to isolate the problem. Jenkins leaves the stage and starts wandering the auditorium in his jammies.

2:30 pm

Weidman approaches Maltby. Can they add a line—something like, "Hi, honey, I'm home"—when Josh's father walks in? Seems okay to Maltby. They go to Ockrent. Fine by him. Ockrent goes to Gemignani to see if it will work musically. Sure. They teach it to John Sloman, who will say the line, and alert Walsh and Levis, who will hear him say it and have to respond accordingly and on time. The new line, "Hi, hon," will go in Tuesday.

7:50 pm

A small crowd is gathering out in front of the Shubert Theatre, unaware that the preview has been cancelled. As theatergoers arrive, a security guard hands out a printed explanation. No rioting ensues, probably because many are actors from other shows, dark tonight. They know that first previews are often iffy.

But money is lost. "It's an expensive cancellation," says Kamlot. "We had $25,000 at the box office at 1:00 and would probably have hit $40,000. However, had we given a shitty show, word of mouth would have spread and it would have had a negative effect later on. It spreads fast, and you don't want 1,500 people saying 'I went to the first preview and it stunk.' So in that respect, it's good that we're not doing the show. You know the expression, 'The show must go on?' Why must the show go on?"

Tuesday, April 9, 1996

First preview tonight. Wagner calls it the Marquis de Sade benefit because only sadists come to first previews.

2:00 pm

Medical update: Moore is feeling better but Jenkins has a throat problem and will take it easy this afternoon. Ockrent

says Robillard has a headache—"I've had it since Sunday" she interjects—and he himself woke up with his heart pounding a little too fast.

2:15 pm

At the back of the theater, Maltby is working on eight lines of lyric that continually elude him. "It's the same thing when you're directing," says Maltby. "It comes down to five or six notes you will give [actors] forever, and they will never get it right. They become classics, usually because you're looking for some subtle joke that nobody gets but you."

2:30 pm

Freydberg stops by. This is the most exciting day, he says. It's the day the show will be seen by a New York audience "that isn't expecting how good it is. They don't know what I know."

7:50 pm

That New York audience, which includes Andrew Lloyd Webber, is now filling the theater. Asked how he feels tonight, Weidman replies that "I have all the appropriate feelings. Anxiety, fear, excitement, relief. Shadings of all those things. It's like this is the last lap."

The creative team is at the back of the theater. Standing in the same spot where she watched *Crazy for You* so many times for so many years, Stroman confesses to alternating waves of nausea and nostalgia.

8:10 pm

The show starts. Audience members laugh at the funny lines and lyrics, applaud the set changes. They clap when Cypher comes onstage, and they clap for the dancing bear. They applaud "Cross the Line" even before the number ends. "It's a lot different being in New York, isn't it?" Ockrent asks.

Breast-touching is back in the script. When people get nervous, they focus on silly things, Freydberg says later. He reports that Feld was in the audience tonight and said only, "They put it back in."

10:50 pm

The performance ends to great applause, with some people standing. Eyler calls it "sensational," and Wagner says the toy executive's enthusiasm has been so strong all the way along it's been almost infectious.

11:10 pm

The cast assembles. Ockrent congratulates them on their "baptism by fire." He calls it a terrific production—"We're red hot now." It seems too long, however, especially during the first act. He asks them to try and pick up cues quickly during the next two performances so that he and his colleagues can get a good sense of where to cut. "The wisdom is to make minimum changes now," Weidman says. "But, on the other hand, the wisdom is to do anything you can to make it better."

Ockrent gets through tonight's notecards quickly. The kids should beam their flashlights at the audience, not at the set, during a set change; the idea is to *distract* the audience, not point out the change. The props department should put jam or something in the caviar bowl, so Josh actually has something to spit out when it's time for the caviar-spitting.

At one point, Ockrent gives Moore a note that leaves her looking confused.

Moore: "I thought I was doing what I was supposed to."

Ockrent: "You are. I'm changing it."

11:20 pm

The cast leaves, and the show's creators talk among themselves about how it went. "That audience was *wonderful*," Long says appreciatively. "It was like everyone's mother was there. I've never seen it like that."

Neither, apparently, has anyone else. "Every place there was supposed to be a reaction, there was a reaction," Weidman says. "It won't always be the case, and you don't want to be fooled. There are things that don't work as well as they ought to but worked better tonight than they should. We're lucky to

have two performances tomorrow, so we can see them before we make changes. Second performances are notoriously terrible, plus it's a Wednesday matinee which will mean a different group of people."

12:00 midnight

The meeting ends, and people exit the stage door to snow flurries. Weidman reads Hemingway short stories well into the night, thinking about tonight's performance and not wanting to go to sleep because it would mean the experience was over. "You're still connected to what made you happy," he says later. "You know that when you wake up, you're connected to the next performance and who knows what that is going to be like."

On this show, it's not a bad philosophy.

Wednesday, April 10, 1996

11:00 am

Creative team meets at Stroman and Ockrent's place, a bright, airy, newly-renovated penthouse in midtown. There are bagels and lox in the kitchen, Ockrent's daughter studying at the dining room table and the usual discussion in the living room.

Ockrent begins with a cautionary note: since the preview was "infiltrated" by producers, friends, and such, it shouldn't influence them too much in any direction.

The director wants to experiment with how the audience learns that Josh is an adult. Currently, Josh wakes up and bangs his grown-up head on the top of young Josh's bunk bed. Ockrent is thinking that perhaps he'll put young and old Josh in bed together, mirroring one another's movements; it builds on a visual gag he employed successfully in *Crazy for You.*

"Pederasts in the audience will have a great time," Maltby remarks. Everyone laughs, after which Ockrent says he'll test the idea at the theater. Maltby again responds, more seriously this time: "It's a simple story. What could we get out of that?" Answers Ockrent: "A laugh?"

11:30 am

Conversation dead-ends at the problematic keyboard dance number. "It almost seems to be insuperable," Ockrent groans. "Which is why we begged that it not be on the poster, not on the TV commercial. It has become our helicopter. It is in the wrong fucking spot in this show—with two people we barely know and a crowd of extras we never see again. The structure is insurmountable, [so let's] pare it away to its best components and not have it overstay its welcome."

Should they scrap the song "The Time of Your Life" that now begins the number? The story line that surrounded it has long since been cut, and a *New York Times* reporter, for one, had thought the song was "cryptic." (Interjects Weidman: "Cryptic. *New York Times*.") Ockrent says that what works so well in "Cross the Line" is the integration of a general idea with a specific. Can they do that here? "Right now it seems like a number for the sake of a number," he concludes. "You need to tell us why the fuck we're sitting here watching this."

Maltby is nodding his head in agreement. "You're right. Again, you're right. It's appalling."

Ockrent's on a roll. They should build on things they have now learned. For instance, Cypher is loved by the audience. Why not use him more? And why not more kids' singing? The sound of the kid chorus is "great" in "Cross the Line." And, repeating something he's said before, why not make more use of all the good voices in the ensemble?

More trims. From music. From dancing. From book. (Weidman clutches his chest: "You're cutting the Liberace line?") They are finishing each other's sentences now. Maltby: "These seem like some very exciting ways..." Stroman: "to make everything land..." Ockrent: "and allow us to learn more about these people."

2:00 pm

Matinee performance. Another sold-out show, plus a line for returned tickets. A happy-looking Freydberg is surveying the crowd at intermission, even interviewing a family or two about why they're there. The producer says Feld was right to

blanket television with ads now instead of waiting for reviews, and one woman shepherding four kids through the lobby readily supports this view. She would have waited for the reviews, she says, but not her kids. They loved the movie, saw the commercial, and were "mesmerized" during the show.

Indeed, perhaps because it's Easter week, perhaps because it's a matinee, the place is packed with kids. At the end of the show, there are so many wrappers and candy boxes on the floor it looks like *everyone* there was under 15. "These kids are the future," Stroman says. "That was one of our main goals with *Christmas Carol*—to see 5,000 kids with their eyes riveted to the stage. If Broadway is going to survive against video, cinema and TV, it will have to be by hooking kids into the theater."

5:00 pm

At the end of the performance, Ockrent heads onto the stage. Not dissuaded by Maltby, he escorts Robillard, a small woman, and a tall male dancer onto the set with the bunk bed to test his idea of having both Joshes in bed together. The bed proves too small to pull it off, so he tries having them stand together, her in front. That doesn't work either. He moves on to the next problem.

Thursday, April 11, 1996

Today's agenda: Polish both first act production numbers.

1:00 pm

Rehearsal starts with "Fun." First problem: should the new lyric be fun "gets you warm when you're cold" or fun "warms you up when you're cold?" The music people feel "gets you warm" sounds clearer. But Maltby isn't sure; he has the singers try it one more time on the piano and then decides "warms you up" makes more sense. They compromise with "warms ya up."

There are new jokes in "Fun" today. As Josh, MacMillan and company dance away on the keyboard, one toy store shopper asks if the piano is on sale. Her friend replies, "I wonder

if it comes with a bench." Nobody laughs at tonight's performance, and the exchange is gone by the weekend.

4:10 pm

Stroman is putting a button on "Cross the Line." Everyone first holds his or her final pose, after which the choreographer has each do the last few steps that precede the pose.
She also reminds the actors that the audience can see them
looking tired or unhappy. "If you have to make a face" she
says, "do it when your back is to the audience."

The music "ride-out" is also key, Shire adds. If it isn't right,
the audience won't know when to applaud, and you can lose
the whole response to the number. Most contemporary pop
songs end by gradually fading out, and that doesn't work in
the theater.

6:30 pm

Freydberg is at B. Smith's restaurant on 8th Avenue to
address a group due at *Big* tonight as a benefit for the Canavan
Foundation, an organization raising money to research the
inherited, degenerative canavan disease. The show's lawyer,
Seth Gelblum, is among the group's founders, and he calls
Big "a Broadway show created by Broadway people." Freydberg
tells everyone his theory that poor reviews in Detroit were good
news, not bad. Shows often get good reviews out of town and
come here and bomb, he says. "They believe their reviews."

11:00 pm

There's a mob at the stage door, and most of the swarm is
female and under 14. When Brett Tabisel comes out, they
scream his name and rush at him. He signs autographs for
more than half an hour and guesses later that he wrote his
name 65 times. He also got his cheek pinched four times. At
the height of the frenzy, leading man Jenkins comes out in a
knit cap and is totally unnoticed. He walks through the crowd
and heads on home.

Friday, April 12, 1996

Another day of doing a dozen things, many at the same

time. Little of the theater is unused, from the stage to the aisles to the foyer of the ladies room.

Moore and Jenkins are each at their respective doctors, and rumors are circulating that either or both could be out tonight. (Neither is.) Jenkins calls in to say the doctor is running behind, and he'll miss another half hour of rehearsal. Ockrent is stupefied by this: "Danny is just too nice," he mutters. "Have [stage manager] Steve call the doctor and say it's an emergency. We can't have our leading man sitting in a doctor's office all day."

After rehearsal, press agent Bob Fennell comes by to get information about the creative team when each was 13. Shire reports he was interested in piano, softball and science fiction. Asked where he was at 13, Weidman shoots back, "You mean in my therapy?" He was interested in sports, he offers, just as Shire reappears: "And I had a magic act."

Maltby put together the Syosset Revue in the 8th grade, noting, "No one in school had a clue of what I was talking about, but they did have a whole assembly with it." He was also intrigued by set design, saying, "My dream was to design scenery for Radio City Music Hall."

Ockrent was a movie addict, especially German art movies. And Stroman? "Tap, jazz, ballet, baton and personality singing."

Maltby, Shire and Weidman now discover they have something else in common besides Yale: all of them went to top East Coast prep schools. "Here we are writing musicals," Maltby muses. "Why aren't we CEOs of major corporations taking golden parachutes? What's wrong with us?"

Monday, April 15, 1996

Big gets six nominations from the Outer Critics Circle, the first group to announce its award nominees this season.

"Going from total silence in Detroit to people laughing and applauding has made me hopeful," says Stroman, "but you can never call it. Before, I couldn't sleep because I was obsessed with fixing the show. Now I'm obsessed with what the response will be, and I still can't sleep."

Adds Ockrent: "We've been through so many emotionally

charged valleys and mountains with this show, it's hard to believe it's not still very problematic. And we can still be crucified. Who knows if we aren't climbing that mountain of false euphoria?"

Wednesday, April 17, 1996

Eyler brings 98 people to the show, including F.A.O. Schwarz store managers from all over the country. "They told me, 'We love the movie *Big*, hoped the musical was as good, and it was even better than we expected,'" reports Eyler. "There was tremendous excitement. This is an extremely engaging attraction."

It's also an extremely complicated one, especially from Zweigbaum's perspective. The production stage manager stands in a 3' by 3' space at the side of the stage and faces monitors that show him what's going on in the orchestra pit as well as onstage. His eyes dart back and forth between the script and cue sheets in his three-ring binder while he talks into a headset and his hands work switches on a board of cue lights. There are 431 light, sound, set and other cues in this show—an average of one every 30 seconds or so.

Suspended nearby are chunks of scenery that move up, down and sideways during the performance, and to his right is a constant stream of stagehands, actors and dressers. A dresser sets up a chair with Jenkins' clothes, readying a change that takes seconds. Portions of the huge, heavy piano are hoisted down, and stagehands adjust them, clean them and load them with small teddy bears. Two huge teddy bears have to be unhooked (and, later, rehooked) from a storage area over Zweigbaum's head before the piano is put in its track and sent onstage.

During one of the special effects, stage fog covers his feet up to his ankles.

Thursday, April 18, 1996

Weidman gets good seats for pal Jonathan Schwartz and family. Radio personality and author Schwartz has been promoting the show on air at WQEW for months.

Schwartz had heard stories about Detroit but says he ignored them. (His father, composer Arthur Schwartz, and lyricist Howard Dietz had written the score for Fay and Michael Kanin's *The Gay Life*, the first show at Detroit's Fisher Theatre.) Schwartz has known Maltby and Shire for several years and had even suggested the two men hook up with Weidman one day. These were three men whose work he respected.

"I'd been plugging the show for a year and a half, even as the fellows were writing it," Schwartz says. "Then, after Detroit, I redoubled my efforts on the radio to balance the gossip scale. I feel that anything that John Weidman considers worthy to spend two or three years of his life on, is something I am going to pay serious attention to."

Now, finally seeing *Big* in the theater, he feels "extremely exhilarated. The first 20 minutes are as good as anything I've seen. It has a lot to say about childhood and how difficult it is to become an adult; it has a lot to contribute. I believed that before, during and after seeing the show."

When the performance ends, Schwartz stops to visit with Maltby, Shire and Weidman at the back of the house. Hearing him praise the show, the authors ask Schwartz to write liner notes for the coming cast album. Schwartz says he'd be thrilled and would have it for them in 10 days. Which he does.

Among his remarks: "Richard Maltby, Jr., and David Shire, a collaboration whose past work has spoken as honestly as Sondheim's about the perplexing and under-addressed corners of the heart, have supplied *Big* with genuine melody and candor of lyric that such a tricky conceit as Kid-Becomes-Big requires. It is a beautiful score, one that will grow inside yourself as time goes by."

Friday, April 19, 1996

Tabisel is in the 42nd St. subway station, en route to class at the Shubert, when police stop him and take him in for questioning. They ask why he isn't in school, and he tells them he's in a Broadway show. "Oh, sure," say the cops. He pulls out his ID card from the Professional Children's School, and, apparently convinced, they let him go.

A street-wise, smart-ass New Jersey kid in the show,

Tabisel is a street-wise, smart-ass New York kid in real life. "If I was back at being 13 again, I would love to have had a friend like Brett," Ockrent tells a TV interviewer. "He was exactly the Billy of all our imaginations."

Tabisel seems comfortable with all the adults, probably because he's been doing this sort of thing for years. He toured 150 cities with *Peter Pan* when he was 9 and even hired his own manager that year. He toured again in *Falsettos* a few years ago, then moved on to television appearances, commercials and now *Big*. He will probably have a television series before he is old enough to vote.

Sunday, April 21, 1996

New York Times Arts & Leisure section has article on *Big*, complete with Hirschfeld drawing, that reviews Detroit problems—technical, dramatic and critical. Writer William Grimes quotes *Variety*, cites a "nonstop mutual massage" between the show and F.A.O. Schwarz, and implies more artistic tie-ins than exist. Freydberg is quoted saying that the toy store appears in just one scene and the curtain call: "If this is exploitation, I'll eat the set."

Monday, April 22, 1996

More press coverage. Last week's *Theatre Week* put *Big* on its cover, and Randall Short's piece on the kids' ensemble runs in *New York Magazine* today.

"Every time I pick up the paper, it seems to be something that assaults us," Maltby remarks. "I feel like we've built this lovely boat, and we have to take it in and dock it on the other side of Haiphong Harbor, and Richard Nixon just dumped 20,000 mines into it. At least, *New York Magazine* saw us as an innovator, bringing youthful energy to the Broadway stage."

Short's article credits choreographer Stroman with giving the show "its distinctive style," and a chat with her father indicates she knows from child dancers. Charles Stroman, visiting rehearsals today, says she was choreographing at six and appearing summers at Tony Grant's Stars of Tomorrow in Atlantic City by the time she was nine. Not only was she "an

angel from the day she came into this world," says her father, "but she was probably in more recitals and parades than any dancer who ever lived."

At first, the choreographer admits, it wasn't as rewarding to work with the young dancers. She didn't get the feedback she does with adults, and it was more like teaching a dance class. But now, she says, "They really understand the process, and it's thrilling for me. They're quite verbal in suggesting things for their characters. They've learned from performing and from being with adults, and they've blossomed into savvy musical comedy dancers."

There was also an unexpected side benefit, she adds. "What it's done for me is reawakened the dance inside of me. When you choreograph, it's all about using your brain. You get awards for what you do with your brain. In doing this show, because the kids started out as dancers, I had to go back myself and get in touch with pure dance. I feel I'm in the best shape, dance-wise, of the last five years in order to keep up with them."

Tuesday, April 23, 1996

Cast has the day off, but everyone's busy at Freydberg's Fremont Associates. There's a recording to plan and opening night seating to worry about.

10:00 am

Maltby and Shire meet in the conference room with record producer Phil Ramone to plan the *Big* CD, set to be released this summer by Universal Records.

Six recording companies expressed interest in *Big* at one point or another. The crowd narrowed as two record companies proposed budgets that were too low, another had financial problems, and another came in too late. Fremont director of business affairs, Ralph Sevush, says the remaining two contenders promised aggressive mass media campaigns to lift *Big* out of the cast album niche. They chose Universal, he says, because it was a new label with experienced executives "and we believed they could focus their attention on this one project."

Universal also came through with a sizeable budget, and how best to spend that money is what's under discussion at this meeting. Swathed in black, both hip-looking and *zaftig*, Ramone has with him performance notes and tapes of the show. Since studio time is limited and expensive, the men want to get as much done as possible before the planned May 6 recording session.

Like the large cast and the major orchestra requirements, the guy who records Barbra Streisand, Billy Joel and Sondheim shows does not come cheap. With a budget of $442,000 (of which about $420,000 will be used) *Big* joins such other big-budget cast albums this spring as those for *Rent* and the revival of *A Funny Thing Happened on the Way to the Forum.* Ramone proposes 77 minutes of potential material (out of a show that runs about 135 minutes) and says they'd be even better off with 60. But the final recording must be meaningful to people who have not seen the show; the first-time listener should have a sense of what's going on.

Maltby and Shire sing aloud much of their score, with Shire working off his music sheets, Maltby from his script. The two men disagree from time to time—"The authors are now squabbling," Ramone observes at one point, amused—but they and Ramone seem to have similar notions of what is essential and what is not.

1:30 pm

Box office advance is $2,568,668, which Kamlot calls disappointing. "My expectations were for much higher than that," he says. "It was based on a successful motion picture, and all of us in this business wear rose-colored glasses. We always think everything is going to be better than it is. But we don't have a star, and we're competing with *Victor/Victoria* which does have a star."

Down the hall, Freydberg has his own anxieties as the show's opening nears. "This period is strange," says the producer. "It's the end of the process of making a show and finding out if it will be accepted by a group of people who haven't the foggiest notion of how you make this happen and are com-

ing in to judge what all of us have done. I find it a very bitter time. I find it physically painful."

As Freydberg speaks, most of his staff is huddled in the company manager's cubicle, redoing the seating chart for opening night. Balanced on a long shelf are two 6' by 3' seating charts—one for the orchestra section, the other for mezzanine and balcony—covered by ¾-inch colored dots. About 10 different colors, augmented with stars or smaller dots, represent authors, producers, agents, staff, press, stars and others.

Several dots are stuck at the top of the board, above the seating sections, and represent people still floating in limbo, waiting to be placed. But 1,437 of the 1,449 seats in the theater have already been allocated.

Needless to say, everyone in the invited audience wants to sit third row center, and producing associate Michelle Leslie is already spending a lot of time arranging and rearranging those dots. Already on her second round of seat assignments today, she expects to be at the office as late as 10:00 p.m. In truth, she leaves at 2:00 in the morning.

Wednesday, April 24, 1996

11:30 am

Press agents gather at F.A.O. Schwarz for a walk-through of the opening night party. They and FAO party planners head down to the lobby, then outside to discuss where they'll put the red carpet, stars and photographers. Among the 15 costumed characters expected at the event is Truffles the Teddy Bear.

They discuss what and when the band will play. (Keep it lively from the start.) Transportation for the stars (limos) and rest of the cast (buses). Best way to handle the ticket booth. (No sales that night. Grant wishes instead.) What to do about people who walk off with *Big* hats as souvenirs. (Let them go. Security people expect it.)

4:45 pm

At the Shubert, meanwhile, Ockrent stands at the center

of more and more concentric circles of worry. Gemignani is the last of several people who stop to ask him something, and the director looks truly distracted. "Do I need to be listening to what you're saying?" he asks his music director.

Filmmaker Martin Scorsese was asked once to define a director, says Ockrent, "and he replied that 'A director was a man who answers questions.' It's also true of directing musicals."

6:00 pm

There's a short, flattering interview with Weidman in the *Daily News* today, and Wagner reads it aloud to everyone over dinner. Next come reassuring stories of people they know—Wagner's daughter, Weidman's mother—who loved their musical. Ockrent says his son has been sending messages onto the Internet about how brilliant the show is.

All are obsessing about the first press performance tomorrow night. As far back as December, Ockrent talked about working several years on a show "and then everything rides on one guy's yea or nay. It's a daunting experience as you see somebody saying, 'Here's the review.' Your heart sinks, and your eye keeps going until you can say, 'Oh, *there's* something good in it.'

It's the end of the process, he says now. "Opening night takes care of itself. The continuity of the show hangs on the reviews and basically one review. If [*New York Times* drama critic Vincent] Canby likes it, we'll have a very good run. And if he doesn't, it doesn't mean it's the end, but it will be an uphill struggle and the producers will have to put a lot of money into sustaining it through what will be a tough time."

8:00 pm

Ockrent watches the show from the seat that Canby will sit in tomorrow night.

Thursday, April 25, 1996

First press performance tonight.

At 7:15 p.m., Ockrent is backstage, encouraging his cast and, it turns out, anybody who crosses his path. "All the best,

guys," he tells the musicians. He hugs his stage manager and his costume designer, plops kisses on the foreheads of his female ensemble, kibitzes with his male ensemble, heads up the stairs to the stars' dressing rooms, rushing in and out. To Jenkins, he paraphrases a line from *42nd Street* —"You're going out a youngster and you're coming back a star"— and he welcomes Cypher back "to your natural habitat."

As crowds push into the Shubert, lighting designer Paul Gallo remarks, "It doesn't matter this time what goes wrong. It has to go right. And it doesn't matter if the show is good. We all know it's good. It's how it will be perceived by the critics. We love it, and I'm passionate about it, but remember, my kids go to school off this show. Its success is vital to my livelihood. They don't call it show art. It's show *business*."

At the back of the theater, Shire and wife Didi Conn are standing still, huddling close, but Stroman, Weidman and Maltby are pacing. Ockrent is crouched on the stairs, pressed against the wall, looking as if he wished he could be swallowed up until the whole awful experience is over. In a few minutes, he will get up and pace as well, back and forth, staircase to staircase, looking for problems and hoping he won't find them.

"So it all comes down to one night," says Shire. "It's kind of savage, isn't it?"

10:30 pm

Show ends. No set problems. Nobody fell off a skateboard. Nothing flew into the pit. "It was a good solid show," Ockrent says. "It was our best shot. That's all we can ask for."

Friday, April 26, 1996

Bring in 'da Noise, Bring in 'da Funk gets a rave in today's *New York Times*. The tap/rap discourse on African-American history, which opened last night, "...not only transferred gracefully (from the Joseph Papp Public Theatre)," writes critic Ben Brantley, but "it now also seems clear that Broadway is its natural and inevitable home. And it is speaking to its audiences with an electricity and immediacy that evokes the great American musicals of decades past."

4:15 pm

Staff meeting at Boneau/Bryan-Brown to discuss who will be where at Sunday's opening night events. Publicist Boneau, who will be in charge, outlines the evening for the 11 staff members who will be at either the theater or the opening night party. Some will baby-sit press, others cast members or celebrities. They expect "a pretty good celebrity turnout," including Sarah Jessica Parker, Matthew Broderick, Jane Alexander and Mayor Giuliani. They will try to get the mayor to wear red sneakers.

8:00 pm

Director Harold Prince and his wife Judy are in the audience tonight. "I thought it was in and out, and some of it very good," he says later. "And that's what I think about most shows I see. Some of it was swell, and some of it wasn't so swell. It was an entertaining musical. But it's all so much luck about when you open and what people think—what people's expectations are."

Saturday, April 27, 1996

Mark has just come in from Phoenix, where the film he is producing—*Jerry Maguire*, starring Tom Cruise—is currently shooting. Like everyone else on the show, Mark is speculating about the *New York Times* review. The *Times* has liked everything lately, he frets. "It's like Vegas. Just because it went heads 12 times, it doesn't mean the 13th time will be tails. And yet, you worry about it. And you start overanalyzing. Like this.

"In Hollywood, if you're involved in a movie that doesn't work, nobody remembers it a minute later, including you. But for some reason, that isn't true here. People have already stopped talking about *Cutthroat Island*, but they're still talking about *The Red Shoes*."

Sunday, April 28, 1996

Opening night tonight. Rehearsal this afternoon.
There are balloons just inside the Shubert stage door, and

the hallway to the production office is lined with gifts that have been arriving since early this morning. There are so many gifts of all sizes and shapes that somebody had to tape people's names to the wall behind their stacks of presents. F.A.O. Schwarz needed a truck to bring over all its goodies, and the kids' dressers had to start stacking their gifts in a stairwell to make room for their costumes.

The last Western Union delivery totalled 35 telegrams. The cast bulletin board is replete with greetings—from the casts of *Victor/Victoria*, *Master Class* and *State Fair*, from individual actors and friends.

3:00 pm

Ockrent is out in the auditorium, slouched in his seat. "I feel kind of resigned," he says. "I expect the worst, and anything better than the worst will be a pleasant surprise. I'm always very pessimistic at these times—it saves me from many horrible moments."

Why have a rehearsal now? "To get everybody's adrenalin up," Ockrent answers. "There are so many first-night presents and other thoughts, it helps concentrate things."

3:45 pm

Ockrent ends the rehearsal. He gives notes to a few people, then calls everyone together for what will be the last time.

"This has probably been one of the longest rehearsal periods any of us have ever had," says Ockrent. "That's the joy, thrill and problem of doing new work and of creating new shows. It's never easy. This show will go on and on, and you will have been there from the beginning. It's now no longer Richard, David and John's show. Now it's your show, and it's up to you guys to love it and maintain it and keep it fresh. Don't ever let it be just a job."

4:30 pm

Gypsy robe presentation. Everybody gathers on the stage, forming a circle. The ornate "robe," a fabric patchwork of logos, visual jokes and titles of recent Broadway musicals, is about to be awarded to Frank Mastrone, who

plays everything in *Big* from a toy company executive to a transvestite. The robe is given on opening night to the ensemble member who has appeared in the most Broadway ensembles, and Mastrone's credits include *The Phantom of the Opera*, *Les Misérables* and *Cats*. It's a custom that began in the '50s and, like so much that happens on Broadway, now a beloved tradition.

Mastrone slips into the robe and passes inside the circle three times as everyone touches his new finery. Then he heads up to the dressing rooms to bring good luck to the rest of his colleagues. Tomorrow night he will take the robe over to his counterpart for the opening of *Rent*.

6:30 pm

Press agents are in front of the Shubert greeting critics and celebrities. Boneau approaches Mayor Giuliani with a shoe box. Inside are red Converse high-tops, immortalized in the show's logo. Getting down on one knee like a shoe salesman, Boneau opens the box and says, "This is the style for tonight, and this is what we're offering in your size, sir."

It works, and 20 minutes later, Giuliani comes onstage in his red sneakers. "This is going to be a very exciting evening and a very important [opening] for a very big show," says the mayor. "It is about New York City, and it takes place in New York City. It's going to be a great, great success. I know it. Just like those New Yorkers who were here for the opening of *A Chorus Line*, you're all going to be able to say, in the future, you were here for the opening of *Big*."

8:15 pm

Intermission. Some reviews written after the press previews are already available, and a few are terrible. Freydberg looks glum.

Ockrent is outside, pacing Shubert Alley like an expectant father. "We were up against it from the beginning," he says. "If you take something people know and like, you have to be brilliant to overcome the preconception of, why bother? You have to say something more, and I believe we do but I'm not sure it's clear enough."

157

He stops and looks over at the *New York Times* building across the street: "All that matters now is what is being printed in that building over there."

9:35 pm

Performance ends to passionate applause, screams, shouts and a long standing ovation from the invited audience.

9:45 pm

Press agents are in the lobby of the *New York Times* building. No papers yet. The paper usually comes up at 9:40, but some days it's late and they have to wait. Tonight they have to wait eight minutes. But as soon as Boneau gets a copy and starts reading, he yelps, "Holy fuck!" He is out the door, in his red sneakers, rushing back to the party.

10:00 pm

Eyler and family are just inside FAO's front door welcoming 1,500 guests. There are tables and a dance band off to the side, and the store is dotted with cartoon characters, toy demonstrations, bars, travelling waiters and food tables. The menu, more kid-oriented than at most such parties, includes "the world's greatest hot dog stand."

As arranged, most of the cast arrive in buses, the stars in limos. Jenkins sticks his head out of the sunroof of his vintage stretch limo and does an impromptu press conference at the curb.

Boneau comes racing in the door, searching for Stroman and Ockrent. He circles the room and finally finds them. He keeps repeating, over and over, "It's a rave. It's a rave."

Stroman grabs his arm and says, "Please, don't kid me." Then she bursts into tears.

Big is a "bright, shiny, larger-than-life toy of a show," writes Canby. "[It is] so exuberantly gifted that it gives you the helium high of a balloon flight....Whatever the collaborators did in Detroit has paid off. Among other things, *Big* is (at long last) an answer to *Beauty and the Beast*."

Canby's last two lines: "It worked as a movie. It works as a show."

11:30 pm

Word reaches Ockrent that Weidman and his family have been in a car accident en route to the party. Mark offers his car and driver, and the two men set off for Roosevelt Hospital. With them are Weidman's brother-in-law, urologist Dr. Norman Coleburn, and sister-in-law, orthopedic surgeon Dr. Cherise Coleburn, who have called ahead to the hospital.

A few minutes later, the white stretch limo arrives at Roosevelt's emergency room, and the formally-dressed party rushes through one hallway after another in search of Weidman. He is in an emergency room cubicle, his tuxedo jacket off, his sleeves rolled up, but still wearing his tie and cummerbund. He is holding a white compress to his bleeding lip.

Weidman tells everyone his family is okay—his daughter's nose bled a lot but wasn't broken—and they tell him about the *Times* review. Ockrent then pulls it out of his pocket and starts reading chunks of it aloud to Weidman. Weidman's wife Lila enters the room, hears about the review, and starts to cry.

Weidman's in-laws stay at the hospital, but a few minutes later, Mark, Ockrent and Shire, who has just arrived by cab, are back in the limo and returning to the party. Ockrent leans back in his seat: "Thank God tonight is over. That is it. I don't want any more of these moments. The roller coaster ride has finally come to an end."

PART FIVE:
AFTERMATH

AFTERMATH

T H E roller coaster ride is not exactly over.

First huge drop is a critical onslaught. The *New York Times* review made for a festive opening night party, but media responses are wildly contradictory.

The best notices are in the two most important publications, the *Times*—because it is the *Times*—and *USA Today*, which reaches the out-of-towners who help carry a show after the first few months. In *USA Today*, David Patrick Stearns calls it "the ideal family musical," finding it the "best-crafted show this side of Stephen Sondheim." Stearns gives the show four stars, noting "few recent musicals have been this lovable."

Other praise is tempered, as in *Hollywood Reporter* critic Frank Scheck's reference to *Big* as "the one new old-fashioned musical comedy of the spring season." Writing in *Newsday*, Linda Winer pegs it "an amiable throw-back—a sweet enough, square enough, simply melodic and well-adjusted family fantasy informed by mall culture, hard-sell Broadway show-biz tradition and Hollywood."

Then come the harsh and sometimes simply dismissive opinions. Critics find the show's bigness and backers unattractive in a season that produces such low-budget, high-minded fare as *Rent* and *Bring in 'da Noise, Bring in 'da Funk*. The show is compared to the film and, often, found lacking. What they had most feared from the start about taking a hit film to the stage is now grist for newspaper and magazine critics.

To *New York Post* headline writers, *Big* is "one 'BIG' bore" and to the *Daily News*, "a 'Big' let down." *The Post*'s Clive Barnes dismisses it first as "the small matter in hand," then as "a pallid entertainment" and a "bemusingly dull evening." The *News'* Howard Kissel feels *Big* "doesn't fulfill its potential;" it has an "essentially mechanical nature" and a second act that is often "a pallid homage to *How to Succeed in Business Without Really Trying*." *Variety*'s Gerard calls it "a long loaf of Wonder Bread in a season rich with grainier fare."

163

Stewart Klein at Fox-TV's Channel 5 considers it "small pota-toes," and for Dennis Cunningham at WCBS/Channel 2, it is a "charmless and joyless enterprise." Gannett critic Jacques Le Sourd calls it "dreadful," labelling it "a show that seems to shoot itself in the foot at every opportunity."

The public is expected to decide for itself when the Tony Awards air June 2 on CBS. Nominees for Best Musical, which few doubt will include *Big*, each get a chance to perform an excerpt from their show on the broadcast. In 1994, Disney was able to sell $1.3 million in tickets to *Beauty and the Beast* the day after the Tonys—despite losing the Best Musical award to *Passion*—and Freydberg can't wait to give *Big* that shot at America's viewing public.

Monday, April 29, 1996

The conference room at Serino Coyne has been set aside for *Big*. Radio spots written late last night are on the air early today. Newspaper and other reviews have been clipped, pho-tocopied and collated.

Neatly-stacked review packets are in the center of the huge conference table, and new reviews are added—and the cover page updated—all morning long. Several television sets are on, soundless, as press people, producers and assorted ad agency staffers move in and out of the conference room. De-livery men bring in breakfast, then lunch.

9:30 am

Press agents are the first to arrive. They read through the reviews and an attached sheet that has culled the best, most quotable lines from each review. Selections for the actual ads change again and again as more reviews come in and more people read them. Boneau calls the *New York Times* review "almost an embarrassment of riches."

Boneau and colleagues strategize; everything will turn with the rave *Times* review. The question now is which stories to plant where. To whom should they pitch feature profiles of Jenkins and Stroman? How should actors and authors be positioned for Tony nominations? What's the best way to get

more television exposure for the kids? Can they maximize the mayor's enthusiastic comments of the night before? Boneau picks up the phone and starts making chatty calls to important reporters and editors.

Mock-ups of the *New York Times* ads for Wednesday, Friday, and Sunday are tacked to the wall for everyone to judge. The Friday ad will wrap around the *Onstage, and Off* column, filling the rest of the page, something Freydberg wanted from the start; it took considerable doing, he tells the creative team later, and he had to pay a premium for it. The more traditional Wednesday ad will run alongside the ABC's—the theater listings—and the Sunday ad will be a full page.

The Sunday ad is not just to sell tickets. It is also to remind the Tony nominating committee—which makes its selections that day—that *Big* is a show worth remembering. The ad will reprint praise given specific actors and authors.

The advertising goal: "While we want to be smart," says Boneau, "we don't want to be cocky."

The advertising quandry: to go with short, quick quotes that look as if they didn't have something good to say or longer quotes they fear that nobody will read.

11:00 am

Copywriters and art directors dart back and forth to their offices, changing layouts, photos, quotes. They want to get the ads as finished as possible before the producers start coming in around noon. At one point, account executive Carol Goren goes to the art director's computer and starts typing in the quotes herself; she's the fastest typist in the place, she says, as her fingers whiz across the keys.

11:30 am

Count so far: seven positive reviews, nine negative, three mixed. While reviews will appear for the next several days, today's pattern holds.

11:50 am

Review packets are off the table and stashed away as pro-

ducers begin to arrive. Only sheets of ad-worthy, favorable quotes are visible.

The *New York Times* and *USA Today* reviews will be heavily featured in ads. So will UPN-9's Pat Collins, who called *Big* the "*Annie* of the Nineties." (Later they will add, and also prominently feature, a column item from Liz Smith calling the show's dancing "the best damn dancing in a musical in a long, long time!")

"We now have an opening," says Feld. "A crack in the door. We have good reviews, and we're on a roll. Now is not the time to pull back. We should take advantage of the heat of the moment."

Mark agrees that the *Times* review is "a money review." Canby also dismissed all the earlier charges of commercialism as well as the Detroit reviews, the producer adds.

12:30 pm

Conversation stops so everyone can watch Joel Siegel live on WABC. Siegel likes *Big*, and the ad execs grab their notebooks. Featured in their Wednesday ad will be his observations of "a big heart, big talent and... a really big show."

1:30 pm

Press agents Boneau and Fennell huddle with Mark to choose and arrange review quotes. After they leave, Freydberg redoes the ads.

Tuesday, April 30, 1996

Meeting today at Ockrent's apartment.

The director has read only the good reviews, but he knows of the bad ones: "I think we were doomed from the early articles of FAO and commercialism, capped with the not good word from Detroit. The reaction was so extreme, it can only be associated with what was viewed as crass commercialism. Once that ball gets rolling in the press, it just permeates everything. Whoever reviews it can't do so except through those glasses. It's like we're not being reviewed as a show but as an event in the theater that is viewed with disdain."

The show itself brought its own demons, as they learned

again and again. Ockrent recalls, for instance, the daunting moment when "I realized that the basic story gave us a lead character who was reactive rather than an active character and my heart sank. It made everything more difficult. Every scene was a problem. I'm not certain we ever overcame it although we came close."

But the director feels it is still too soon for him to make an intelligent appraisal of their show. "It takes a while before I can look at it objectively. The recovery time, even if it were an unqualified smash, is three or four weeks."

12:50 pm

Freydberg arrives first. The producer can't wait to share news of the forthcoming advertising campaign. He tells Ockrent the producers plan to sponsor the news broadcast following the Tonys and may even run a commercial locally during the awards show as well. Then he opens his briefcase and pulls out the Friday ad that will wrap around the theater column in the *New York Times*. "I got this weeks ago," he says excitedly. "I paid a premium."

1:15 pm

Maltby and Weidman arrive, and Freydberg shows them his ads. He also outlines the rest of his advertising—the radio and television ads are averaging maybe $90,000 a week, the print ads another $100,000 a week. He has a budget of $678,000 for the next three weeks, he boasts: "This is the single largest ad campaign any musical has ever done. And if we win Tonys, we will really go big. We will do what they've been accusing us of doing. We will become very commercial."

Weidman, who looks worried, gets out of his chair and starts pacing the living room. The television ads concern him, he says; what he and his colleagues created onstage is not apparent in the content-free, montage-style format of the television commercial. The show Canby praised in the *Times* is very different for Weidman from what is in that commercial.

But Freydberg is talking business now. "You have to do that to sell tickets," he tells Weidman. "It's $70 a pop. Broadway is Las Vegas. It is a tourist business. The commercial

167

sells tickets. I thought we would do $150,000 a week during previews. We did $368,000, $400,000 a week."

Expect a Hyundai tie-in later, the producer hints.

2:10 pm

Everyone moves to the den, a comfy room filled with his-and-hers photos, plaques and window cards from Ockrent and Stroman's shows. The group listens to a tape of Maltby and Shire's proposed record album, decides it is fine, and moves on.

3:10 pm

Tony talk. What production number should they do on the nationally-televised show, given this is their very best chance to sell tickets to America? They review several possibilities. The keyboard number, "Fun." Perhaps "Cross the Line." Maybe something cinematic like a tight shot of little Josh becoming big Josh. They decide to decide later.

3:30 pm

Freydberg heads back to his office. In the car he confides that if *Big* had not received the *Times* rave, the show "was in danger of closing. We would have had a couple weeks with enough of an advance that we wouldn't be losing too much. But then we would have had trouble unless we had a lot of Tony nominations. And without that review, we probably wouldn't have. That's how close it was."

He himself would probably have gone out of business, he adds. "I have no other shows running. This is the first time I don't have other things ready for production. I have no other income, and I have a big staff."

4:30 pm

Freydberg calls the Shubert box office. He listens, then hangs up the phone and says, "They're convinced that if you have a rave, there will be a line around the block. But that's from the '30s. They didn't build Rome in a day. They didn't even build *Cats* in a day. That's why they say, 'It's building'

when people talk about box office."

7:15 pm

Ockrent is back at the Shubert. He's soon off to London, then on to Italy with Stroman for their long postponed honeymoon, so he's saying goodbye to his actors. Zweigbaum will maintain the show, he tells each one. Zweigbaum, whom he has known for 10 years, "is strong and brilliant." They should feel free to go to him with any problems.

When he and Stroman return, Ockrent says, he'll come again to see them and the show.

Wednesday, May 1, 1996

More reviews. More post-mortem.

Out-of-town critics mirror hometown extremes of positive and negative. *Philadelphia Inquirer* critic Clifford A. Ridley calls *Big* a show with "an observant eye, an agile brain and a generous heart." But *Detroit News* reviewer Kenneth Jones likes the show even less on Broadway than in Detroit, saying it "has the eager tang of a PBS musical special about puberty." Laurie Winer at the *Los Angeles Times* calls it "disappointing" as well as over-choreographed and over-directed; she disdains the score, and says the keyboard number "has no more authentic joy than a TV commercial for the toy store, which by the way is one of the show's producers."

Shire expresses surprise at the tenor of the bad reviews. "I thought if critics didn't like the show, they would say it was inconsequential," he says. "But these are vicious in their dismissals. You'd think the show is about something controversial like abortion or Christian fundamentalism. Something about this show, beyond what is up there, is pushing their buttons."

The composer agrees with Ockrent that early coverage of *Big*'s merchandising set a tone from the start, minimizing the show's content and maximizing its marketing. "By the time we opened," says Shire, "the industry had been primed to see the show in that way. Maybe I was naive, but I thought negative reviews would be blander, that we would be damned by faint praise."

Instead, he continues, "a surprising number of critics totally missed the show Richard, John, Susan, Mike and I thought we were presenting—the mythic aspects, the rite of passage, the contrasting points of view of adults and children— and focused only on its commercial aspects. Somebody could say, 'That's your fault as an artist for not making it clear enough.' But other critics saw it. People we know saw it. The audience saw it. Their reviews made it sound like a cynical, exploitative, superficial entity, and that isn't what we were writing in any way."

Thursday, May 2, 1996

Big gets 10 Drama Desk nominations—tying with *Rent* for the top spot. Robin Wagner, nominated for both his *Victor/Victoria* and *Big* set designs, is upset that Ockrent is overlooked. "Nobody would even be there if it weren't for Mike Ockrent," says Wagner. "They don't really know how shows are made."

It is also opening day for the Broadway Show League in Central Park, where *Big* plays *A Funny Thing Happened on the Way to the Forum* on Diamond 3. The *Forum* team leans toward comely courtesans, but the *Big* team boasts powerful male stagehands and athletic females.

By the end of the first inning, the score is 6 for *Big*, 1 for *Forum*. The game is stopped at the end of the fifth inning when the score is 26 to 2, invoking the league's "mercy rule"—if one team is leading the other by more than 15 points after 4 innings, the game is stopped.

There will be other times at bat. As one actor from *Forum* tells a friend in the *Big* company, congratulating him on the *Times* review: "It looks like we're all going to be around a long time."

Friday, May 3, 1996

Freydberg, who swears he doesn't read reviews, has now at least heard about most of them.

He, too, feels that the F.A.O. Schwarz relationship has had an enormous impact on reviewers and is, says Freydberg, "ter-

ribly misunderstood as something it wasn't. But if I had to do it again, would I do it? Yes, I would, and in most seasons, it wouldn't have meant a damn thing. But in a season where several small shows from off-Broadway come in [with such success], there's a backlash against the heavy commercialism of the last few years. We became an example of what the press no longer wanted to see on Broadway—the large, successful, mass appeal show."

His partner Feld, who produces essentially review-proof circuses and ice shows, could not care less what critics say. Even at the opening night party on Sunday evening, he spoke of the *New York Times* rave as "a plus" rather than a milestone. "The reviewers have never been of concern to me," he said that night. "I'm so used to getting beat up by the critics, I never would have gotten into this if I thought it was contingent on the critics. I went into it because I loved the property and the people involved."

Look at the bigger picture, Feld says now. "When I see that the public responds so well to the show, I figure as long as the audiences like it, there's got to be a way to sell it to them."

Just give him time.

Saturday, May 4, 1996

4:00 pm

Freydberg is in the subway when a water main breaks, starting a major flood. "Water is pouring down the stairs, like an avalanche, and I'm thinking, 'Oh, my God, the box office tonight and tomorrow will be destroyed.'"

11:00 pm

At the Shubert, producing associate Michelle Leslie and her boyfriend, Len Ostroff, have gone backstage after the performance. Leslie thinks they're to talk with their prospective landlord. Everyone else backstage knows that the landlord isn't there; her engagement ring is. The couple arrives at the stage manager's station, and Ostroff hands Leslie a rose, gets down on one knee and asks her to marry him. "Please say

yes," he pleads, "and do so quickly. I'm going to pass out." (She does. He doesn't.)

Monday, May 6, 1996

Tony nominations come in this morning, shortly before the start of an all-day recording session for the show's cast album.

8:00 am

Robert Kamlot gets on the subway headed for Sardi's, the show business restaurant that hosts the announcement of Tony nominations each year. He has been on the nominating committee himself in recent years, and he always attends when he has a show on.

This year Kamlot has high expectations. He figures *Big* will receive at least seven nominations: best musical, direction, choreography, score, book, a few of the performers.

8:30 am

Sardi's is standing room only. Tables have been pushed aside, and the room is packed with dozens of producers, publicists, media people and others. A half-dozen television cameras up front point at the podium where Patti LuPone and Matthew Broderick are about to announce nominees for the 50th round of Tony Awards.

The first award category announced is Best Performance by a Featured Actor in a Musical, and nominees include young Brett Tabisel. Within minutes, Stroman receives a nomination for best choreography. Weidman is nominated for best book, Maltby and Shire for best original score. Moore is among the nominees for Best Leading Actress in a Musical.

LuPone and Broderick are on Best Musical now. The nominees are announced alphabetically, and the first is *Bring in 'da Noise, Bring in 'da Funk*. A few people look around quizzically. There's been a mistake; somebody mixed up the alphabetical order. But the next nominee is *Chronicle of a Death Foretold*. Then *Rent*. Then *Swinging on a Star*. There has

172

been no mistake.

Kamlot's mouth hangs open. "I'm shocked and stunned," he says. "I'm absolutely dumbfounded. It is incredible to me that there are people who considered *Swinging on a Star* or *Chronicle of a Death Foretold* more worthy of a nomination than *Big* or *Victor/Victoria*."

The company manager is hardly alone. There is now an audible buzz in the room. Several other people are also standing listless, their mouths open. A reporter rolls his eyes at another reporter. *Chronicle* ran only 66 performances. *Star*, which ran 115 performances, was a revue of Johnny Burke songs. Both long ago closed. What is going on?

It is a sweep for Off Broadway and the non-profit arena, with *Rent* receiving 10 nominations and *Bring in 'da Noise* nine. All four Best Musical nominees originated in non-profit houses, as did all four nominees for Best Play. The 14-member nominating committee, whose members include playwright Jon Robin Baitz, costume designer Donald Brooks, choreographer Marge Champion, writer Brendan Gill, and set designer Ming Cho Lee, has definitely made a statement.

Victor/Victoria receives only one nomination—for Julie Andrews as Best Leading Actress in a Musical—and left out at *Big* are everyone from Ockrent and Wagner to Jenkins and Cypher. The show's five nominations are fewer than the seven that Maltby and Shire's *Baby* received more than a decade ago.

11:15 am

Meeting at Serino Coyne. Mock-ups of newspaper ads are on the conference room table when press agents arrive, and Freydberg is already there studying them. Coyne and other ad executives read aloud the likely radio and television spots.

Freydberg gets Feld on the speaker phone, then places the instrument at the head of the table where everyone in the room talks to it. Coyne again reads aloud the planned radio and television ads. Freydberg doesn't want decisions made while they're angry, and neither does Feld. "Let's take the positive side of this," says Feld's voice on the speaker phone, "and play to our strengths."

Coyne can't contain her wrath, however. "I'm shocked not just on your behalf but for the industry," she says, in a passionate monologue. "Who will watch the two-hour show? Broadway never had a better season, and they're leaving off [*Victor/Victoria*'s] 'le Jazz Hot' and [*Big*'s] piano number? Why didn't someone say, 'Think about what it will look like on TV? Think about how this will affect the industry you love.' These are not the theater awards. They are the Broadway awards. These people didn't shoot themselves in the foot. They shot themselves in the head."

12:20 pm

Back at Fremont Associates, Freydberg is on the phone to *USA Today*'s Stearns. He is pacing furiously, back and forth, as far as his phone wire allows. "Not being on the Tony show is a serious loss for us," he tells Stearns. "You can bet CBS wants Julie Andrews singing on that show, and if she does, I want my piano on, too... I never heard of a show being nominated for best score and best book and best choreography but not best musical. It is not just us. But not nominating *Victor/Victoria* which has been running to full houses all season?"

Down the hall, Kamlot has his own analysis of the situation. "The committee leans to the left theatrically and is a very anti-establishment group," says Kamlot. "I'm distressed we did so poorly and further distressed we won't be on TV and that we won't win anything.... But I'm not casting any aspersions on the committee. I served with them for three years."

12:45 pm

Lunch break at the Hit Factory, the ultra-sleek recording studio where Universal has been recording the *Big* CD since 9:00 this morning. Over pasta, fruit and salad, talk turns to the nominations.

"Are the Tonys a reward for artistic achievement or are they a commercial for Broadway?" asks actor Ray Wills. "That's the question. If the Tonys are to promote Broadway, then why [choose] two nominees that already closed? People can't come

see them. And if they're about high artistic achievement, that's subjective and 14 people decide it."

Tony nominee Tabisel jokes that his mom is probably passed out on the floor right now, but he seems subdued. Yeah, he's excited, he says. Sure. But he's sad about the people who didn't get nominated.

So is fellow nominee Weidman. The playwright is particularly upset that Jenkins received no nomination, he says later. "Danny is the head of the company, and it sets a tone, particularly given the kind of work we had to do in Detroit. It's very demoralizing he wasn't nominated. It's demoralizing the show wasn't nominated."

2:50 pm

Cast members are mostly in the lounge area, reading newspapers, picking at wilted salads, playing cards. A production assistant comes by to round people up for "Cross the Line," the number that ends the first act.

In the enormous recording studio, the orchestra is gathered several yards away from the cast, which is itself divided into groups of adults and children. Microphones are everywhere. And on the other side of a wall-length window, the musical team, recording staff and assorted visitors listen to take after take of songs destined for the cast album.

3:45 pm

Twenty-nine minutes are now recorded. The session will continue until midnight, and the final album will run just over 65 minutes.

Tuesday, May 7, 1996

New York Post headline today is "Tony Baloney." *Daily News* refers to *Big* snub, and *New York Times* refers to "the back-of-the-hand treatment accorded *Victor/Victoria* and *Big*."

The nominations are "frightening," says Freydberg. "They say an investor can put up a large amount of money, get favorable reviews in the right places, and get a nominating committee with an agenda."

Out in California, producer Mark is perplexed. "It would be easier to buy a total shutout," he says. "You assume they hate you and you live with that. This makes no sense. What were they thinking?"

He figures the show got caught in a trend toward smaller shows. And the irony, recalls Mark, is that before the sets were built, the producers were worried that *Big* was too small. It was a time of big-budget European imports, and they wanted to be competitive with shows like *Les Misérables*, *The Phantom of the Opera* and *Miss Saigon*.

In retrospect, he says, "We would have gotten credit for pitching a tent and having a couple of guys playing Jew's harps. They would have said, 'Look what they managed to do for 12 cents.'"

Freydberg agrees that both the critics and the Tony nominating committee "were rebelling against a big musical. They wanted something that wasn't so big. Something original, not revivals or musicals from movies. They looked at us and said, 'This may be good, but it's more of the same.'

"If *Big* isn't a hit, it won't have anything to do with the show. It will have to do with the state of the business when the show came in. This is a hit show. The audiences love it."

He himself loves it. "People have no sense of the commitment we had to this and what we were doing—not to make a fortune but to work together and make something happen. But in the end, we've been punished. The fact that Mike [Ockrent] and Dan Jenkins and the show were not nominated is more painful than any loss I would personally have. You can make money back, but it's very hard to heal a broken heart."

For Feld it is a call to arms. "The first tendency is to get into this whole brawl and feel it's unfair. But the reality is that life's not fair, so you have to go with what your assets are. The good news is that we set ourselves up as if we were a hit. This is a letdown, but I don't want to roll over and die. I love to overcome obstacles. I love a good fight."

Wednesday, May 8, 1996

Julie Andrews ends the matinee performance of *Victor/*

Victoria with a short speech. She tells her audience—and, soon, all the world—that she is declining her Tony nomination.

Victor/Victoria is a collaboration, says Andrews, and her collaborators "have been ignored by this year's nominating process." Rather than accept her nomination, she will stand alongside her husband Blake Edwards, the show's director and librettist, as well as her fellow actors, designers and other colleagues—"the egregiously overlooked."

Thursday, May 9, 1996

Big kids assemble at Times Square McDonald's on Broadway in their *Big* T-shirts to perform a few minutes, pose for pictures and sign autographs. The appearance helps kick off the new Arch Deluxe burger as well as a promotional tie-in between *Big* and the food chain's New York outlets.

Saturday, May 18, 1996

Big kids host and perform at luncheon gathering of presenters from around the country who might book the show on tour.

Several of the kids complain about the tiny stage—which one compares in size to a compact car—but they are making so many promotional appearances these days that small stages will soon become very familiar.

Sunday, May 19, 1996

Drama Desk Awards are presented at the New Victory Theatre. Although *Big* had received 10 nominations, a number equal to that of front-runner *Rent, Big* wins no prizes tonight. *Rent* and *The King and I* sweep musical awards.

Monday, May 20, 1996

Variety prints Critics' Tally for *Big*: four positive reviews, six negative, six mixed.

New York Observer critic Rex Reed comes to *Big*'s defense in today's paper. Ignoring *Victor/Victoria* and *Big*, he writes, "was a clear declaration of war against the kind of classy, traditional musical shows Rodgers and Hammerstein

used to write." He has his reservations about the show but concludes his column saying "*Big* may not be big enough for the Tonys, but it's still the best family show in town."

Tuesday, May 21, 1996

Weidman has finally had enough evenings free to go to the theater and catch up on all the other musicals.

His conclusion: "*Bring in 'da Noise, Bring in 'da Funk* at its best was thrilling. *Rent* was exhilarating. By which I don't mean more thrilling or more exhilarating than our show. My son Jonathan, who's seven, is obsessed with basketball and always wants to know who's better—(Orlando Magic's) Shaquille O'Neal or Penny Hardaway? I tell him they are different kinds of players, and it's exciting both are on the same team. And that's the way I feel about this."

Friday, May 24, 1996

Outer Critics Circle awards ceremony at Sardi's at 10:30 p.m. *Rent* receives award as best Off Broadway musical, and *Victor/Victoria* receives award as best Broadway musical. Julie Andrews receives the award for best actress in a musical and comes by Sardi's after tonight's show to receive her scroll and make a few remarks.

While *Big* had received six nominations, it receives no awards. However, Outer Critics Circle long-time president Marjorie Gunner sent her daughter, son-in-law and two of her grandchildren to *Big* prior to the awards ceremony. They just adored it, she says.

Saturday, May 25, 1996

Broadway is booming with some of the best-received plays, musicals and revivals in years.

What's good for audiences, however, isn't always good for producers. *Bring in 'da Noise, Bring in 'da Funk*, *Big* and *Rent* opened not long after critically-lauded revivals of Edward Albee's *A Delicate Balance* and Rodgers and Hammerstein's *The King and I*. So many appealing shows have come in at the end of the season, in fact, that they are splitting the audience. Nobody's making a profit, says

Freydberg, and everyone's worried about July, traditionally a slow time. Including him.

"I think if there weren't so many shows on Broadway right now that were successful, we would be doing $550,000 to $600,000 a week instead of $400,000 to $425,000," the producer says. "People line up at the discount ticket booth, and it's eliminating the full-price ticket. We're selling 80 to 85% of seating capacity but only 65% of dollar capacity.

"There are 12 musicals at the booth. Many have stars, and we don't. Others were nominated for best musical, and we weren't. That's a pretty tough sale."

Tuesday, May 28, 1996

More Tony coverage. Columnist Michael Musto chastises Julie Andrews' "vituperativeness," writing in the *Village Voice:* "I applaud Julie's nerve, but you can't get mad every time someone you think deserves an honor doesn't get one or Jennifer Jason-Leigh would be a serial killer."

Sunday, June 2, 1996

Tony awards at the St. James Theatre. "Who knew the Tonys could push LaToya Jackson off the front page of the *New York Post*?" asks host Nathan Lane in his opening monologue. "Welcome to the tabloid Tonys."

Welcome, too, to the unstoppable Tonys. The broadcast survived David Merrick's legal challenge—the producer had sought an injunction, unsuccessfully, to assure that all and not just some of the songs from *State Fair* would be considered for Best Original Score—as well as the possibility of a strike by stagehands.

All the attention also resulted in not just increased sales for *Big* and *Victor/Victoria*, but invitations to appear on the broadcast despite being overlooked for Best Musical. *Victor/ Victoria* declined, but *Big* and *State Fair* accepted. *Big* fills its 1 minute 45 seconds with the piano keyboard number, but neither it nor any of the other musical excerpts look particularly inviting.

Indeed, nothing on the show comes across particularly well. To insure that the show doesn't run more than its allot-

ted two hours, some awards have been presented, and taped, before air time. As a result, taped and live segments are thrown together, making it look at times as if people don't even recognize their own names when they are announced as winners. Even very short acceptance remarks are cut off abruptly. Lane is wonderful when he is on camera, but he doesn't appear often enough to save the show. An awards show heralding one of the best seasons in recent Broadway history falls flat on national television.

Rent receives four Tony Awards, including Best Musical, and so does *Bring in 'da Noise, Bring in 'da Funk.* Tony voters take Julie Andrews' words to heart and do not award her a Tony, honoring instead Donna Murphy for her work in *The King and I.*

Big receives no Tony awards.

Monday, June 3, 1996

Nominee Stroman, who has won Tony awards at two prior ceremonies, still feels sad about last night's event.

"I felt that the creative people on the Great White Way had finally given Broadway what they'd been asking for—a show for a rock-and-roll audience, a black audience, for lovers of Rodgers and Hammerstein, people who adore musical comedy and people who love revivals. But instead of the 50th year being celebrated for its diversity, the shows were pitted against one another, and there was a mean spirit in the air.

"All the people who worked on *Big* are the people who devote their lives to the theater and feel a great responsibility in creating new works. Broadway this season was rich with many styles and should have been celebrated for that."

Tuesday, June 4, 1996

The mixed reviews and Tony snub are taking their toll. At the Shubert, daily box office sales have dropped by half since the Tony nominations, Freydberg says, meaning that the show's advance is also down.

Freydberg is now "panicked" about July. *Big*'s entire advance for the month is $200,000. If *Big*'s grosses drop below

$320,000 for two consecutive weeks, he says, the Shuberts have the option on their "stop clause" to ask *Big* to leave.

Andrew Lloyd Webber's new musical *Whistle Down the Wind* does not yet have a theater locked up, and the British composer has been casting a covetous eye at the Shubert. Even if *Big* survives July, it could do so losing a large amount of money. Should the show then be forced to close later, the Shuberts would lose not just *Big*'s business but *Whistle Down the Wind* because the theater would not have been available to Lloyd Webber.

"They're positive we will hit the stop clause," says Freydberg. "My question is if we do hit it, will they try to close us? Their dilemma is an obligation to us as well as an obligation to Andrew, who has had more long-running hit shows with them than anybody else in history. If the Andrew Lloyd Webber situation didn't exist, this wouldn't even be an issue. But they can't promise him the Shubert, and they can't promise us that they won't close us."

Neither he nor Feld want to close prematurely, says Freydberg, "but we are prepared to do so if things don't change, and the Shuberts rightfully pointed out to us that our odds are not good. All we want is our chance to turn it around so that both the investors and the creative staff have a fair chance at a success."

The producers decide to focus their marketing efforts on July. They will introduce a "July Sale"—a discount plan by which tickets purchased for July by June 30 would be $25 off. They will start selling a "family pack" of four balcony seats for $125.

Wednesday, June 5, 1996

The League of American Theatres and Producers releases season-end figures. Broadway ticket sales went up 7.3% to $436 million, and 82% of those dollars were for musicals. The Broadway audience in the 1995-96 season (ending May 26, 1996) was 9.4 million people—the highest number in 15 years—and 76% of them were attending musicals.

In other news, the *New York Times* reports that Tony show ratings were the lowest ever, down 35% from as recently as

1993. The awards show lost out in its first hour to NBA play-offs and in its second to a *Matlock* rerun.

Thursday, June 6, 1996

Freydberg and Feld decide to pursue what works so well with the circus and Feld's other attractions—aggressive marketing.

They order one-million discount coupons to distribute in not only Manhattan but also Connecticut, New Jersey and other outlying areas. The coupons will offer the same $25 off in July, plus half-price tickets for the week of July 4. They will be sent through the mail as well as distributed at corporations, in stores and neighborhood shops.

Monday, June 10, 1996

Creative team agrees to defer royalties until at least the end of July. Suppliers of lighting, sound and other technical equipment consent to lower rental fees for a while. Freydberg says that Feld would cover losses and additional advertising "if everybody else participated in some way, and that was a way to do it. He didn't feel, and rightfully so, that he should foot the whole thing himself."

Thursday, June 13, 1996

Freddie Gershon, chairman and owner of Music Theatre International, talks with agent Flora Roberts, who is representing the authors, about licensing *Big* for amateur productions.

"I think this show was partially destroyed by the review in *Variety*," Gershon says. "It set the tone that this was a piece of crap and brought out the *schadenfreude* in everyone. It isn't good enough that you succeed but that your friends fail. Everyone was rooting for it to die. And it wasn't an event either, because of Jonathan Larson's death and the advent of *Rent*. Then came *Bring in 'da Noise. Big* was perceived as 'old-fashioned, passé, why Broadway sucks. Feh. *Big* is symbolic of everything old-fashioned that we don't want on Broadway.'

"I feel this show in any other year, in any other season,

would have found an audience. It is a remarkable set of cir-
cumstances; their stars were in the wrong astrological con-
figuration. *Big* should have gone the *Jekyll & Hyde* route; if
they had gone city to city, [like the new musical *Jekyll & Hyde*]
they would have been on the Internet, people would have ex-
changed 'hits' and *Big* would have come into New York critic-
proof."

Gershon, who saw the show in various incarnations, ac-
knowledges that *Big* has problems and feels it worked best at
890 Broadway, in the rehearsal hall. "It was so much clearer
at 890," he says. "It had everything going for it. What's frus-
trating to me is that I know this could have been more than it
is, and I don't know where it went off. You had five not just
talented but super collaborative people, and from the minute
it went up in Detroit, it wasn't the same show I saw that left
New York City. I don't know if it was working around sets that
slowed them down and made it cumbersome, but the heart
of the show was lost."

Yet, he continues, "the music is there, the characters are
there. I wish it were better, but it is good enough, and I have
every intention of acquiring the subsidiary rights. I feel this
show will be done by my middle-America market. I think they
will have fun with it. It's a great community theater show.

"If I had the choice of licensing *Rent* or *Big*, I'd rather be
licensing *Big*. It can be done in Australia, in London. It will
find its audience outside of a very jaded, overly-sophisticated,
very trendy New York City. New York City doesn't have the
pulse of America."

Friday, June 14, 1996

Freydberg is quoted in the *New York Post* and on the
United Press International wire denying rumors that *Big* is
closing. The producer also offers, presumably in jest, to give
up the Shubert if Lloyd Webber is willing to give him the Ma-
jestic, the theater in which *The Phantom of the Opera* is playing.

Saturday, June 15, 1996

Freydberg goes to the discount ticket booth in Duffy Square

for the second time this week and interviews people in line about what shows they want to see. He finds out they want to see *Big*, but there are several shows they want to see more. *Big* is rarely their first choice.

Worse still, *Sunset Boulevard* tickets are now also available at the TKTS booth. *Big*'s ticket sales are drastically affected by this newest competitor, he says, claiming that they dropped from over 400 a day to 150 once *Sunset* entered the picture. Now he hears that *Show Boat* might also start releasing tickets to the discount booth, and he worries even more.

Freydberg decides he better come up with more discount programs to circumvent competition at the booth. So in addition to the family packages and July discount coupons, he adds a new wrinkle—the personal approach. Over the next two weeks, his assistant Douglas MacArthur will train 25 young people to promote *Big* to tourists. At the end of the month, they will fan the city, heading for such local tourist spots as South Street Seaport, Rockefeller Center, ferry docks, museums and hotels. Potential theatergoers will be told about the wonders of *Big*, then handed the discount coupons for July.

"We're telling them, why go to the ticket booth and stand in line in the heat?" says Freydberg. "They don't have to pay cash like they would have to pay at the booth. They can use their credit cards to buy tickets by phone or at our box office.

"The object is to not compete directly. We put ourselves in first position."

Tuesday, June 25, 1996

Greenblatt and Feld come in second at the Dellwood Country Club member-guest golf tournament, but who cares? *Big*'s box office business is headed upwards—today's take alone is $104,000, Greenblatt enthuses—and an advertisement this Sunday will announce that tickets are on sale through December 31.

"Everything that should have happened without the political bullshit is happening," says the indomitable Greenblatt.

"We're going to beat the Broadway political insiders that tried to ruin this show. The audiences will not allow it to happen. They're coming in droves in spite of the industry."

Wednesday, June 26, 1996

Richard Maltby has been informally "investigating" the Tony nominations, and he is very disturbed by his findings.

While he had initially been upset by the show's snub, Maltby says, he wasn't really "galvanized" into action until he was at the Tony awards and saw an excerpt from *Swinging on a Star*, a show he hadn't seen previously.

"It was a nightclub number," says Maltby. "And I thought, 'This is odd.' Why did 14 distinguished members of the theater community prefer that show to one that got a rave in the *Times* and that audiences seem to love every night? It just didn't jibe."

It made him remember back to an event at the Mayor's mansion a few days before the Tony Awards. He ran into a friend there who was on the Tony nominating committee, and "the friend immediately volunteered that he loved *Big* and preferred it to *Rent* and had voted accordingly."

Intrigued, he decided to call some other people he knew on the committee. "I asked people to tell me not how they voted, but where did we go wrong. Did they think the show off-base from the minute the curtain went up? Did it go 10 minutes and take a terrible turn? Did we promise something we didn't fulfill? Clearly we had offended these people in some way that was a mystery to me."

To his surprise, Maltby says, he found that almost all of the people he called were very enthusiastic about *Big*. "And this, of course, made me feel pretty good, because there was no great antagonism to the show."

But their responses led him to what he calls "a second mystery: The same people who were so enthusiastic about *Big* went out of their way to mention that they had not voted for *Swinging on a Star*. If that was the case, why was *Swinging on a Star* nominated instead of *Big*?"

The lyricist, who also creates word puzzles for *Harper's Magazine*, began to track the numbers. Taking into account

the weighted voting—four votes for first place, three for second, etc.—Maltby did some math.

"*Big* received three second-place votes, four third-place votes and one fourth-place vote for a total of 18 points," Maltby says. "Conversely, eight committee members did not vote for *Swinging on a Star* at all, and a ninth voted for it in fourth place. Since there wasn't a tie, the remaining five voters of the 14-member committee had to produce 18 votes for *Swinging on a Star.*

"Mathematically, no less than three people *had* to vote for *Swinging on a Star* in first place, and the other two vote for it in second place. The alternative is four first places and one third place.

"I can't imagine that in a year of *Rent* and *Noise/Funk,* five people would have voted for *Swinging on a Star* in first or second place. And if they didn't believe it was the first or second best show, then they must have voted for it simply to skew the voting.

"*Big* didn't get the nomination it deserved because five people voted improperly. That is the story the numbers tell. Why they did it, I have no idea. I believe that a crime got committed here, and I personally am one of the victims."

Maltby says he spoke with Jed Bernstein, executive director of the League of American Theatres and Producers, who "told me it was water under the bridge. It was not nefarious. I say his head is in the sand."

Not yet satisfied, Maltby drafts a letter to Bernstein and Isabelle Stevenson, president of the American Theatre Wing, which presents the Tony Awards. "I was persuaded by my producer and collaborators not to send it," he says, "because they feared it could only bring negative publicity to the show."

His findings obviously continue to disturb him, however, (and lead Maltby to contribute his letter for this book's appendix).

Thursday, June 27, 1996

The American Theatre Wing and League of American Theatres and Producers announce a new nominating committee for the 1997 Tony Awards as well as changes in the nominat-

ing process. The Tony nominating committee size is expanded to between 15 and 30 members from its previous 9 to 18. The entire 1996 committee has been asked to serve again, and an additional 14 members have been named, among them Robert Kamlot, a former member and the general manager for *Big*.

Nominators are now limited to one three-year term, with one-third of the committee changed annually. (The 1997 committee members will be assigned one-, two- or three-year terms in a drawing.)

Weighted voting has been eliminated.

Friday, June 28, 1996

Today's *New York Times* reports the expansion of the Tony nominating panel. Freydberg is quoted as calling for an investigation of voting that, he says, was done "to make sure certain people and shows were not nominated."

Columnist Peter Marks says no investigation seems likely, and League executive director Bernstein later confirms that none occured. Freydberg is meanwhile named to the Tony Awards administration committee which oversees rules and administration of the awards.

Sunday, June 30, 1996

Sam Shepard's play, *Buried Child*, closes today. More relevant to *Big*, so does Rodgers and Hammerstein's musical, *State Fair*. Some of that audience is expected to go to *Big*.

Tuesday, July 2, 1996

Big cast album is released. F.A.O. Schwarz launches the album with a short performance by cast members and a CD signing. Planetariums are now on sale in the *Big* shop, and boxer shorts are expected later this week.

Tuesday, July 9, 1996

Big makes it through the July 4 crunch. There were 21 shows at the discount booth, says Freydberg, "but it didn't matter. We had lines at our box office of people with coupons."

Although producers managed to come in $54,000 over the $320,000 stop clause, Freydberg wasn't taking any chances. When Feld wanted to get two tickets for *Big* that week, his partner didn't pull out complimentary tickets; he paid for the tickets himself.

Wednesday, July 10, 1996

Shire is back at the Shubert to see *Big* after several weeks away. "I found myself looking at it very dispassionately, a little like Oliver Sacks' anthropologist on Mars," he says later. "At times I asked myself of all the different versions we had, why is it this one that is finally there as opposed to one of the other myriad permutations. Was this the best of all the versions?

"I thought of Jerome Robbins' remark that musicals are never finished. They are abandoned. Time runs out, and you open with the version you have at that moment."

Friday, July 12, 1996

New York Times On Stage, and Off column previews the fall season. A scarcity of available theaters has left many musicals "waiting and circling, like 747s stacked over La Guardia."

The "jumbo jet in a holding pattern" is Lloyd Webber's *Whistle Down the Wind*, his first collaboration with director Harold Prince since *Phantom of the Opera*, writes columnist Marks, noting Lloyd Webber seems "to have been stymied by a box office rebound by *Big*." Freydberg is quoted saying their reduced-price sale was a success, and the advance is at $3 million now.

There have been many rumors, Freydberg says later—including one that he was offered $4 million to leave the Shubert, which is "absolutely untrue"—and says his advertisement that tickets were on sale until year-end was a way of dashing some of those rumors. He also says discussions regarding the theater were "on a very high, gentlemanly level at all times. Nobody ever did anything high-pressure or unethical. As much as the Shuberts wanted Andrew Lloyd Webber to have his way, there is no question that they wanted us to succeed just as

much."

Since opening, *Big* has not fallen below 70% in audi- ence, but it has fallen below its weekly break-even point of $380,000. The week of July 1 through 7, for instance, when the audience level reached its highest point yet of 87.4%, box office hit just $374,054, several thousand dollars be- low break even.

Never mind, shrugs the producer. The further they get from the Tonys, the better the audience reactions. Their latest exit polls found that 81.5% who saw *Big* "would definitely recom- mend it," and 74.6% found it to be better than they had ex- pected prior to seeing it.

"So we know that if we get people in there, they love the show. The trouble is that it's tough to get them in there. Which is why we went to discounts."

Wednesday, July 17, 1996

This time it's Feld reviewing the numbers.

At one point, he and Freydberg were talking about losses as high as $800,000 in July, Feld says. Now he expects to lose closer to $50,000 and possibly break even.

Feld credits sheer perseverance. "Many shows, when some- thing happens or they have a bad month, say they're closing. Or they fold up. So they never get the chance to get over that hump. The reality is that summertime is very difficult."

It didn't hurt, of course, that he kept pouring in money— new marketing funds total upwards of $1.5 million over an already high budget. He's planning more promotions in Sep- tember, another weak month, but forecasts a turn-around in late September. "We'll start recouping my additional advertis- ing investment then," he says. "By October, we'll truly estab- lish ourselves. We'll be rolling into the holiday season and next year with a very strong, substantial show."

His goal is to keep *Big* going on Broadway long enough to assure a national tour, possibly as early as fall, 1997. "The ability to run this thing for a year or more in New York gives you the ability to tour it successfully," he says. "I think it has tremendous appeal for the road, and that was always one of the things that was intriguing to me.

"My feelings haven't changed about the show. What I thought early on is what I think now. It is the primary reason why I am devoting a tremendous amount of effort and money. The product is good. Everyone who leaves that theater has had a great experience. The problem with Broadway is that if you sell out, you're still only playing to 11,000 people a week. Word of mouth doesn't travel as rapidly as when the circus or ice show plays to 15,000 people a day.

"Virtually everybody in the business had basically given us up for dead. Now it's starting to get its own momentum. If we're able to turn this around, which it looks like we are, the satisfaction is unbelievable."

Friday, July 19, 1996

Freydberg has maps of New Jersey and Long Island out on his desk. An audience survey found that 29% is coming from New York-area surburbs, and he's thinking about some outdoor advertising there.

The show's 100th performance is next Wednesday. He needs to order a cake and plan some remarks about how well things are going now.

And then? "I have absolutely no idea," Freydberg says. "I go to bed at night hoping I'll sleep fast so I can get up again the next morning and see what's going to happen with *Big*."

190

Autumn, 1996

At press time, *Big* was completing its fifth month on Broadway. Young Patrick Levis, too mature now to play Josh, had been replaced, and a few other cast members had also moved on.

Meetings had begun for a national tour in fall, 1997, but the Broadway production was clearly winding down. Audiences were averaging under 700 at the 1449-seat Shubert Theatre, and one actor lamented that he could see pigeons in the second balcony. Although tickets were on sale through the end of the year, Freydberg conceded, "We're living week by week."

The show posted a loss of $114,000 one week, $188,000 the next, with no indications of the turn-around that Feld had predicted. Advertisements in the *New York Times* declared "final weeks."

In late September, producers announced that the show would close on Broadway on October 13, after 23 previews and 193 regular performances. *Big*, the musical upon which so many dreams had rested, could become one of the most expensive failures in Broadway history.

Appendix

ACKNOWLEDGEMENTS

I would like to thank Susan Stroman for first telling me about *Big*, Robin Wagner for suggesting this could be the show for me to follow and Mike Ockrent for making it possible. Without the cooperation of Ockrent and James Freydberg, not to mention their tolerating an inquisitive reporter at their sides for weeks on end, this book would not exist.

I'm similarly grateful for the cooperation and candor of David Shire, Richard Maltby, Jr., John Weidman and Paul Gemignani, other members of *Big*'s creative team who were very generous with their time and with whom, like Ockrent, Stroman and Wagner, I shared many a fast, tense and, often, dreadful meal in Detroit and New York. The show's producers—Freydberg, Kenneth Feld, Kenneth Greenblatt, Laurence Mark and F. A.O. Schwarz executive John Eyler—were also agreeably open to my continual presence and persistent queries.

The cast and crew of *Big*, whose names follow on the accompanying lists, shared with me their experiences, successes, worries and dreams. While this book eventually concentrated mainly on the show's creation and marketing, I am greatly indebted to the many backstage people who were so patient in explaining terms and in guiding me around cables, quickly moving sets and exiting actors. Janice Jackson, Douglas MacArthur and Nancy Robillard were incredibly helpful, and there is no adequate adjective for Michelle Leslie, my liaison to *Big* and a tireless source of constantly changing meeting times and places, as well as other crucial information.

For their willingness to provide important background for me in interviews on this book, I would like to thank Dori Berinstein, Jed Bernstein, Lynn Bowling, Steven Chaikelson, Didi Conn, Nancy Coyne, Michael Eisner, Larry Gelbart, Freddie Gershon, Ocean Gray, Bernard Jacobs, Robert Kamlot, Fay Kanin, Steve Canyon Kennedy, David Krane, Ron LaRosa, Richard Lee, Ronald Lee, Vivien Leone, Vinnie Liff, William Ivey Long, Anna-Lisa Medeiros, Ray Marston, Gregory Meeh, Harold Prince, Charles Reynolds, Flora Roberts, Gary Ross, Elizabeth Rossi, Gerald Schoenfeld, Ralph Sevush,

Jonathan Schwartz, John Shivers, Arthur Siccardi, Scott Traugott, George Wachtel and Steven Zweigbaum.

An accurate history requires numerous research materials. I'm most appreciative of assistance provided by the League of American Theatres and Producers, and especially publicists Kiley Robertson, Jim Byk and Keith Sherman. I would also like to note help from Richard Kornberg and Don Summa at *Rent*, Carol Fineman and Thomas Naro at *Bring in 'da Noise, Bring in 'da Funk*, Susan Schulman at *State Fair*, Jim Randolph and Bill Evans at *Crazy for You* and Peter Brown for Andrew Lloyd Webber. I am particularly grateful to Shirl Harris at the Fisher Theatre in Detroit, and nearly everyone at Boneau/Bryan-Brown—notably, Chris Boneau, Bob Fennell, Clint Bond, Jr., and, most notably, Patrick Paris.

For their good suggestions, good listening and encouragement on various aspects of this book's writing and publishing, I would like to thank Susan Grode, Malcolm Kaufman, Grace Glueck, David Rintels, Leo Sachar, Paul McKibbins, and, most of all, Stephen Sansweet, Angela Rinaldi, Frances Lear and Elaine Dutka.

My indefatigable agent, Susan Ramer, continued to believe in this book when few others would, and my publisher, Limelight Editions, took the risk. I am most grateful to Limelight's Mel Zerman for that decision, as well as for his wise editing of this book, to his administrative assistant Jenna Johnson and to copy editor Tracey Douglas. Patricia Mattick, my incomparable assistant, provided invaluable editorial, organizational and computer savvy.

Two final acknowledgements. Bernice Kert, a gifted writer and generous friend, graciously read my manuscript and made many smart and incisive comments. Richard Schickel, my loving partner and accomplished mentor, also brought his keen intelligence and writer's eye to this book. Despite his own pressing deadlines, he was never too busy or tired to provide that last bit of advice, encouraging word or elusive adverb.

Barbara Isenberg
July 25, 1996

THE CREATIVE TEAM

Mike Ockrent .... Director
John Weidman .... Book
David Shire .... Composer
Richard Maltby, Jr. .... Lyricist
Susan Stroman .... Choreographer
Robin Wagner.................... Set Designer
William Ivey Long.............. Costume Designer
Paul Gallo .... Lighting Designer
Paul Gemignani................. Musical Director
Douglas Besterman .... Orchestrator
David Krane .... Dance Music Arranger
Vincent Liff .... Casting Director
Ron LaRosa .... Casting Director
Steven Zweigbaum .... Assoc. Director/Prod. Stage
                                     Manager
David Brian Brown .... Hair/Wig Designer
Ray Marston .... Wigmaker
Steve Canyon Kennedy ...... Sound Designer
Ginger Thatcher................ Assistant Choreographer
David Peterson .... Associate Set Designer
Vivien Leone .... Associate Lighting Designer
Scott Traugott .... Associate Costume Designer
Lynn Bowling .... Wardrobe Supervisor
Terri Purcell...................... Assistant Wardrobe Supervisor
Arthur Siccardi .... Production Supervisor
Gregory Meeh .... Special Effects Designer
Charles Reynolds .... Magic Consultant
William Schmeelk .... Shrinking Mechanism
                                     Construction
Rick Baxter .... Lighting Supervisor
John Shivers .... Production Audio Engineer
William Sweeney .... Property Master
Brian Besterman............... Electronic Music/Sequencing
                                     Designer
Patrick Brady .... Additional Vocal Arrangements
Nicholas Archer .... Associate Conductor
Paul Pizzuti .... Percussionist

Peggy Serra .... Music Preparations Supervisor
Robert Wilson .... Children's Guardian
Eleanor Scott .... Tutor
Clifford Schwartz .... Stage Manager
Ara Marx .... Assistant Stage Manager
Tamlyn Freund .... Assistant Stage Manager
Nancy Robillard .... Assistant to the Director
Janice Jackson .... Production Assistant
Douglas MacArthur .... Production Assistant
and many others

THE PRODUCING TEAM

James B. Freydberg .... Producer
Kenneth Feld .... Producer
Kenneth D. Greenblatt ...... Producer
Laurence Mark .... Producer
John Eyler .... CEO, F.A.O. Schwarz
Robert Kamlot .... General Manager
Steven Chaikelson .... Company Manager
Michelle Leslie .... Producing Associate
Elie Landau .... Assistant Company Manager
Ralph Sevush, Esq. .... Director of Business Affairs
Chris Boneau .... Boneau/Bryan-Brown
Bob Fennell .... Press Associate
Patrick Paris .... Press Associate
Clint Bond, Jr. .... Press Associate
Nancy Coyne .... Serino Coyne
Matthew Serino .... Serino Coyne
Rick Elice .... Co-Creative Director
Carol Goren .... Account Supervisor
Regis Albrecht .... Account Supervisor
Tina Braun .... Account Executive
Tom Callahan .... Senior Copywriter
Jim Miller .... Art Director
Glenn Gesang .... Art Director
and many others

THE CAST

(in alphabetical order)

Joan Barber	Ensemble
Lori Aine Bennett	Big Kids
Graham Bowen	Big Kids
Clent Bowers	Ensemble
Joyce Chittick	Dance Captain/Ensemble
Jon Cypher	MacMillan
Brandon Espinoza	Big Kids
CJay Hardy	Ensemble
Rex Hays	Swing
Stacey Todd Holt	Dance Captain/Swing
Daniel Jenkins	Josh
Samantha Robyn Lee	Big Kids
Patrick Levis	Young Josh
Spencer Liff	Big Kids
Lizzy Mack	Big Kids/Cynthia Benson
Donna Lee Marshall	Ensemble
Frank Mastrone	Ensemble
Jill Matson	Ensemble
Joseph Medeiros	Big Kids/Swing
Corinne Melancon	Ensemble/Swing
Crista Moore	Susan
Jan Neuberger	Ensemble/Miss Watson
Kari Pickler	Big Kids/Swing
Enrico Rodriguez	Big Kids
Alex Sanchez	Ensemble
John Sloman	Ensemble
Brett Tabisel	Billy
Frank Vlastnik	Ensemble
Barbara Walsh	Mrs. Baskin
Gene Weygandt	Paul
Ray Wills	Ensemble

Fax from John Weidman to Mike Ockrent on January 17, 1996, regarding script changes.

Weidman says when he was listening to the show, all he seemed to hear were the foul words. So he decided to take some of them out. He calls this fax "Expletives Deleted."

Opening scene, 1-1-3. *LITTLE JOSH*. Cut "Shit!" when computer screen flashes. Replace with pissed off groan.

Opening scene, 1-1-12. *LITTLE JOSH*. Cut "Shit!" when you slam the skateboard down. Replace with "Leave me alone!"

Office scene, 1-6-49. *PAUL*. Replace "back-stabbing little shit" with "back-stabbing little snake."

Office scene, 1-6-51. *PAUL*. Replace "that little scumbag" with "that little weasel."

Party scene, 1-6-68. *PAUL*. Cut "Shit!" when you miss the cookie jar. Replace with "Damn!"

Party scene, 1-6-68. *PAUL*. Replace "you little prick" with "you little jerk."

Coffee Black scene, 2-3-15. *BIRNBAUM*. Replace "Shit!" with "Damn!"

Four friends scene, 2-4-35. *NICK*. Cut "Shit!" Replace with pissed off shout.

Memo distributed by Mike Ockrent at March 9, 1996, meeting in Detroit

General Thoughts:

We need to get under the skin of JOSH more. In song. What we have from him is: BIG. I Want to Go Home. Fun. Stars. Coffee Black and his BIG reprise. None of these songs (except maybe the BIG reprise) gets *inside* him. Helps us know him. We know Susan now. She has Here I Go Again, Dancing All the Time and Special Man. We have really begun to get inside *her* head. Now we must get inside Danny's. What does he feel? Really feel. It's all very superficial. Even though he's a 13 year-old we have set him up with PATRICK as a smart 13 year-old. That's what makes him *special*. Interesting. He's not a *dumb* kid. We must, I think, see more of [his] uniqueness in a grown-up world.

A To Do List:

1) Opening. Rewrite. Consider orchestration differentiating more clearly the adult vs. the kids' world.

2) BIG. Rewrite.

3) Office: re-organize. Order; Susan and Paul. Establish the affair. Set up the meeting. Bring Josh into this mix. Introductions. Bring in Mac plus execs. The toy is dumped after Josh makes a smart kid-like response to the toy... Everyone leaves except for JOSH, SUSAN and PAUL. Get Josh out. PAUL and SUSAN plot. SUSAN sings. Add to JOSH a *smartness*. Make him the only one there who understands the nature of toys... Susan glimpses this. Helps us understand what she will see in him.

4) Loft: Add to Billy scene a sense of where Josh is. Does he still want to go home here? It doesn't seem so. Therefore we have no sense from PORT AUTHORITY on that Josh *wants or needs* to go home. It is all going just swell so we have NO TENSION. Now [that] we have lost the Mother letter, we have no memory of his home or concern for his mother... All care has vanished - all thought of home has vanished. In the latter part of the scene, with SUSAN, we need to add an attractiveness to JOSH here. Maybe STARS does this. Keep Magic

Castle. But give it a better set-up in JOSH/BILLY scene.

5) Write a closing Act I sung by Josh and adults. Danced by kids. Maybe the song also clarifies his inner self in some way that we understand and makes us *care about him more*.

6) Make Special Man special about JOSH. Help us understand what she sees in him. Maybe: *you showed me stars...*

7) Make reprises in the last scene land.

8) Are we happy with MUM coming in at the end of the show?? Is there some other way we could play the very end out?

List of dumb toys sent by John Weidman to Robin Wagner as possible props.

Weidman says the list "was gleaned from earlier drafts of the script. Some of them appeared in sales pitches for new toys, so they include dumb sell copy to go with the dumb toy."

Humpty Dumptruck: A lovable truck with a goofy face that falls apart and <u>can</u> be put back together again.

Rudy Toot Toot: A musical one-robot band programmed to play ten popular songs including "Itsy Bitsy Spider," "Skinamarinkadinkadink" and "Feelings."

TeddyBlare: A combination teddy bear and boombox.

Badger Buddies: The MacMillan Toy Company's failed attempt to compete with "Pound Puppies" and "Care Bears."

Henny Penny: Scratch your way to savings with this barnyard bank. Feed it five cents, it lays a nickel!

G.I. Joanne: Requires no description.

The Dino-Mighty Fossil Factory: Hours of fun for pre-school paleontologists as they assemble their own species of daffy dinosaurs, like the "WhoopsHeSaurus!"

Li'l Baby Poop 'n' Scoop: The anatomically correct action doll you toilet train at home, potty and Play-Doh included.

Clodzilla: The dopey dinosaur that explodes itself into extinction.

Hmmm, that's Gouda!: The miniature dairy farm that makes real cheese.

List from set designer Robin Wagner of Big *mall signs.*

Current Names (Broadway)	**Formerly** (Detroit)
Au Croissant	Au Bon Pain
Buck Rogers	Roy Rogers
Pizza Pete	Pizza Hut
Bonnie Bagels	Dunkin' Donuts
Sprinkle-Dip	Haagen-Dazs
Popsies	Popeye's
Veggies	Subway
Mendy's	Wendy's
Burger Country	McDonald's
Stargate's	Starbucks
Mayfields	Mrs. Field's
Cow Bell	Taco Bell
King Burger	Burger King
Nation's	Nathan's
Barros	Sbarros
Fish N Chips	Baskin-Robbins

Completed songs for Big, *as compiled by David Shire.*

SONGS NOT USED IN THE SHOW

Thirteen

I'm a Kid

I'm a Kid II

Big (replaced after Detroit)

I'm a M-O-T-H-E-R

Say Good Morning to Mom (cut, put back in, and cut again in
   Detroit)

No Problem

Like a Grown-up (cut in rehearsal)

Welcome to MacMillan Toys

My Secretary's in Love

There Goes That Music Again

Office Romance (replaced during rehearsal period)

I'll Think About It Later (put in and replaced in Detroit)

You Don't Want to Know (tried and replaced in Detroit)

The Product

Little Yellow Duck

A Little Fun

Office Quartet

My Very Best Friend

Let's Not Move Too Fast

Turning Into Something

Isn't It Magic? (replaced after Detroit)

Not Quite in Love

Little Susan Lawrence

March to the Music

You're Only Young Once

She Kissed Me (cut in rehearsal)

Move (cut in rehearsal)

Cross Over the Line (predecessor of Cross the Line)

Wha' Da Kids Want?

At the Mall

Happy As I'll Ever Be

Your Choice

The Ballad of Pound Ridge

The Twelve Toys of Christmas

What Is This?

At the Right Time

To Be a Man

Through the Eyes of a Child

Growing Pains

Now I Really Know

We're Gonna Be Fine

SONGS IN FINAL SCORE

Can't Wait

Talk to Her (Carnival Music)

This Isn't Me

I Want to Go Home

Fun (Dr. Deathstar) (Executive Angst)

Here We Go Again

Stars, Stars, Stars

Cross the Line

It's Time

Stop, Time (Happy Birthday, Josh)

Dancing All the Time

I Want to Know

Coffee, Black

The Real Thing

One Special Man (Skateboard Ballet)

When You're Big (Stars Reprise)

Unmailed letter from Richard Maltby, Jr., to Jed Bernstein, executive director of the League of American Theatres and Producers, and Isabelle Stevenson, president of the American Theatre Wing.

I am the lyricist of the musical *Big*, one of this year's new Broadway musicals. I'm quite proud of it, so you can imagine my reaction when *Big* was not included among this year's Tony award nominations for best musical, while two shows that had closed, *Chronicle of a Death Foretold* and *Swinging on a Star*, were. I did not see either of these shows so I have no opinion of them, but the press and the theatre community seemed as surprised by the nominations as I was. It is not my purpose here to characterize any other show. Suffice it to say that to be passed over for these two shows meant to me, as a writer, that the members of the Nominating Committee didn't just prefer other shows, they must have seriously disliked *Big*.

It seemed odd.

At the Shubert Theatre every night, I hear the sound of an audience having a terrific time at *Big*. Believe me, I can tell the difference. Now, when audiences love a show and it gets a rave in the *New York Times*, that show usually gets a Tony nomination. Indeed, it's the kind of show that often wins. I have always prided myself on being able to understand the critical and audience reaction to my shows, even when it's negative. But the discrepancy baffled me. How could my perception of the show on the stage be so different from the opinion of fourteen distinguished members of the theatre community? The show must have antagonized people in ways I didn't understand - and if I were ever to write another show, I felt I needed to understand.

So, after the Tony Award ceremony, when all the dust had settled, I decided to call some members of the nominating committee. I called not to ask them how they voted; I know the nominating ballots are secret. I called to ask them where we went wrong. Did the show turn them off from the moment it started? Did we have them for the first ten minutes and

then somehow lose them? Did we set up an expectation, then somehow fail to deliver? I thought perhaps their responses might unlock some flaw in the show I had missed, perhaps even indicate something we might do to fix it.

The responses I received surprised me. Most of the members of the committee were enthusiastic about *Big*. They "loved it," "really liked it," found it "wonderfully entertaining," thought it was "terrific." They went into detail. They singled out the writing, the choreography, members of the cast. A certain show-stopper here, a writing moment there. When I stopped them and encouraged them to tell me candidly what they didn't like, even to small details, they had very little to say. Responses varied of course: one nominator did as I asked and told me exactly why he had disliked the show; and another spelled out reservations about the show while indicating he had voted to nominate it anyway. But on the whole, there was genuine enthusiasm for *Big* among this committee.

One might ask: Were they telling me the truth? Perhaps they were embarrassed to tell me to my face what they really thought. This of course occurred to me. But it's my experience that when a writer asks theatre people for an honest reaction because he is considering rewriting, they tell the truth. The awards were out. They had no reason to be circumspect. And their enthusiasm and their singling out of details did not sound to me like flattery.

In fact, they did more than praise *Big*. Some volunteered to tell me exactly where they placed *Big* on their voting list. I didn't ask. Most expressed some sort of surprise at the shows that were nominated. I got the distinct impression that many of the committee members were eager to have it known that the list of nominees did not reflect their opinion - even though all expressed respect for the other members who obviously felt otherwise.

Another surprising fact emerged as well: Leaving aside *Chronicle*, which had some strong supporters on the committee, there was almost no support for *Swinging on a Star*. There was even one voter who told me nothing about his ballot except that *Swinging on a Star* was not on it.

208

The enthusiasm for *Big* made me feel good, as you can imagine. But with each favorable response, and each voter who had definitely not voted for *Swinging on a Star*, an obvious question began to arise:

If so many people liked *Big*, and so many people did not vote for *Swinging on a Star*, how did that show receive enough votes to get nominated?

I decided to do some mathematics. As you know, each committee member votes for four nominees in each category, with the votes weighted: four points for the first choice, three for the second, etc.

I spoke to nine of the 14 committee members. I know the votes of two others from second-hand sources. Three I did not contact. From these conversations I have determined the following:

At least eight members of the committee voted for *Big*. Three members voted for it in second place, over *Rent* (nine points total), and four voted for it in third place (eight more points). One voted for it in fourth place. (One more point.) This is a total of eighteen points minimum. It might be more because I don't know the votes of five members.

By contrast, eight of the fourteen committee members did not include *Swinging on a Star* on their ballot list. Of the six remaining members, one had the show in fourth place, for one point. The five remaining voters are the ones whose votes I do not know. Since there was no tie, these five votes must have accounted for eighteen points. Assuming that all five of them listed the front runners *Rent* and *Bring in 'da Noise, Bring in 'da Funk* in first and second place, and all five listed *Swinging on a Star* next, over *Chronicle*, and the three commercially initiated shows, *Big*, *Victor/Victoria* and *State Fair*, that would have generated only ten more points for a total of eleven points.

If *Swinging on a Star* cannot have received more than eleven points and *Big* cannot have received less than eighteen, mathematically *Big* should have received a nomination.

What could have produced the actual outcome?

For *Swinging on a Star* to have been nominated and *Big* not, it must have received at least 18 votes from among the five voters whose positions I don't know. The only mathematical possibilities are: three voted for *Swinging on a Star* in first position (12 votes), above both *Rent* and *Funk*, and the two remaining voted for it in second position (6 votes); or four voters voted for it in first place (as their choice as the season's Best Musical) and the fifth in no less than second place.

That is what the math says. There are no other alternatives.

Now, if three, four or five committee members actually thought that *Swinging on a Star* was the most distinguished musical of the season, I have no argument with them. I might personally question their taste, but if that is their honest opinion, that is fine with me.

But if three or more members did not vote their actual preferences, in order, as the rules direct, and instead gave high voting positions to shows they did not believe were best, for the sole purpose of taking advantage of the weighted voting and skewing the outcome, then I am very upset.

Worse, if three, four or five members spoke to each other and decided in advance that they would collectively vote a certain way in order to manipulate the outcome, I would feel outraged.

And one has to say, it would have to be an incredible coincidence for three, four or five committee members independently and without consultation to give a first or second position vote to a show that eight other members did not even include on their lists.

Did a small number of committee members vote in collusion? What else do the numbers seem to say? And if anything like that happened, I would feel more than outraged, I would feel personally wronged. It would mean *Big* was deprived of a nomination it actually deserved, and that *Big* unfairly received a public statement that it was unworthy of a nomination when

in fact the majority of the committee thought it was.

The committee members I spoke to all expressed total confidence in the integrity of the other members. It was my impression that committee members take their obligations very seriously. I can only imagine what they would feel if it proved that the vote was anything but completely fair.

Why would any committee member not vote his or her actual preference? I have no idea. No member has anything to gain personally by altering the outcome of the voting. Other than the arrogance of affecting the vote, I don't know any reason why anyone would care enough not to vote honorably. I don't want to accuse anyone of anything. Yet something is undeniably odd about the nominations for Best Musical of 1996.

I believe this requires an investigation. I'm sure an investigation is unprecedented, but that should not stop it from happening. It would be an easy matter to poll the committee members, either by phone, or, to keep the secrecy of the ballot, by asking the members to submit their list of Best Musical nominations unsigned in an unmarked envelope by mail. It was my impression that many members would welcome being asked. They too would like to know how this vote happened.

I understand that all the committee members have been invited to serve again next year. Should it prove to be true that a few members set out to manipulate the vote in 1996, I don't believe those members should continue to be on the committee.

If I am wrong in any of the conclusions I have drawn, I will be happy to apologize for this letter totally. If, however, an investigation reveals that the nomination vote for best musical was tainted, I believe *Big* deserves an apology from the Tony awards. That would go a long way toward reversing the unfavorable publicity that the omission produced.

In closing, I want to repeat that I do not intend anything in this letter to be an attack on any other show. I wish all the nominated shows well. Having directed *Ain't Misbehavin'*, I know how high the intentions of a revue can be. I know *Swinging on a Star* is about to embark on a tour, and I do not wish

to denigrate that show in any way. I regret having to mention any other show by name.

But I believe no one in the theatre will benefit if a tainted vote is allowed to stand unchallenged.

Wishes of Big *Kids.*

During a classroom exercise at the Shubert Theatre, tutor Eleanor Scott discussed the theme of wishes in *Big*. Kids were asked to make a list of wishes - anything that came into their heads. Here are some wishes that several of them chose for inclusion in this book:

Samantha Lee
> To win the lottery
> Don't let anything give me bad luck
> I wish there was more room to write at the end of a piece of paper

Joseph Medeiros
> To fly
> To be tall
> To be able to see out my apartment window

Kari Pickler
> I wish to have a mud pie
> I wish I had my license
> I wish I was closer to my friends geographically

Enrico Rodriguez
> I wish I had more freedom
> I wish all my friends lived next door
> I wish I was a little older - preferably 18

Lori Bennett
> I wish the show has a very long run
> I wish all of my friends could come see the show

Lizzy Mack
> I wish I could read people's minds
> I wish my best friend Beth didn't have to move
> I wish my hair was curly
> I wish I had nothing to wish for

Bobby Wilson (children's guardian)
> I wish that the adult cast members would grow at the same rate as the kids, so no matter how big they get, the kids will still look like kids and not have to leave the show

Eleanor Scott (children's tutor)
> I wish I didn't have to leave the play in May
> I wish I was cranking in my studio (sculpture)
> I wish I could be more patient
> I wish I could live on a beach
> I wish my carpet was clean

Patrick Levis
> I wish hair didn't have any style
> I wish love wasn't just a word
> I wish *Big* could run so long that I could be Big Josh

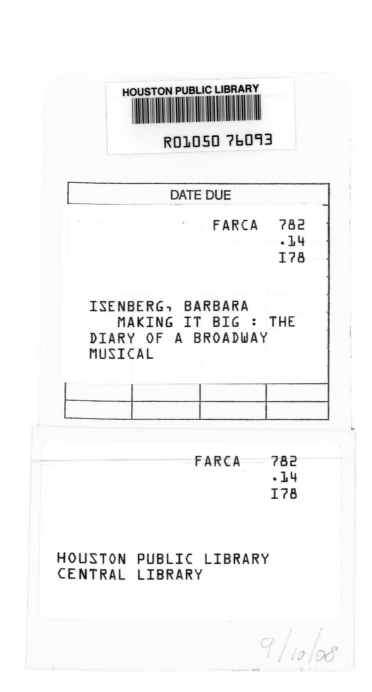
9/10/08